How to Get Here

ABBEY CASTOR

LifeRich Publishing is a registered trademark of The Reader's Digest Association, Inc.

LifeRich Publishing books may be ordered through booksellers or by contacting:

LifeRich Publishing
1663 Liberty Drive
Bloomington, IN 47403
www.liferichpublishing.com
844-686-9607

ISBN: 978-1-4897-3168-5 (sc)
ISBN: 978-1-4897-3169-2 (e)

Print information available on the last page.

LifeRich Publishing rev. date: 11/17/2020

Contents

Foreword

I WANT TO THANK my Dad for always being my number one support system in my life. I owe my ability to travel in the first place to his dedication and love for me and my sister. To my mom for always loving me unconditionally and being there for me no matter what. To both of you who helped to raise me and my sister into the people we are today. I love you both. To Julie who stepped into my family's life raising our awareness about mental health, nutrition and planting the seeds I needed to heal. To my sister, for being you and growing into a beautiful angel.

To all my supportive friends and second family. I could give endless amounts of credit to all the people surrounding me in my life who helped and challenged me to find my voice and find my place in the world coming into who I am. I am eternally appreciative and grateful. I am so happy to have met the beautiful souls that exist in this cosmos and I CAN'T WAIT to meet many more. Let love and light guide us all. I know that by sharing and living out my story that other people will wake up to the spirit of the universe and bask in all its joy, and pure love. I started to doubt myself. Thinking I was crazy for wanting to keep writing this. My friends and family at home would think I was absolutely nuts if I tried to tell them some of what I was going through. But I gave up on caring what they, or anyone else would think. I know how alone I felt while going through all of this. I understand that part of the journeying process IS made through being alone. Being alone is different than feeling alone, and no one should have to question whether their reality is delusional because they are feeling something unexplainable and extraordinary. If my story can reach someone who feels the same, then I accomplished my mission. If this story can reach someone who does not quite understand, but they want to understand then I accomplished my mission. If this story seems magical, and too good to be true then let it inspire you to create your own magic and become the wizard in your own life. We are all capable of accomplishing and wielding the wand of life. Something I have learned from interacting with so many people from all over the world is that everyone wants a chance to share their truth but so many people are afraid of what others might think of them. We lose our creativity when we fear that others might laugh at what we have created. This is my truth with all of my meraki. Amor Fati.

I

Coming home to the Self

SMILING, CONFUSED, AWESTRUCK at how life could be so fucking good. I almost deleted these words several times when I was unconfident about what even felt 'good' about writing this story anymore. Then I added the word fuck and felt satisfied. It's just a WORD. Let me make that very clear in these first few sentences that words are words. We decide to give them meaning then understand what we will with them. Words give us courage. The words we encounter may be encouraging or discouraging for us, but we choose to experience it how we want to. For some people, the word fuck might be slightly discouraging and make them feel a little uncomfortable. For the others, they might be encouraged to keep reading because it excites them to see this fiery swear word fly out on the first page. My intention, for all the words on all the pages I write, is meant to be encouraging. I truly believe that every single being on this earth is capable of stepping into their greatest potential. What is our greatest potential? It is anything that we could dream up. Anything we could put in a movie, we can create. I sit on a painted stool while a cool breeze slowing down the heat

1

of the afternoon brushes across my skin stopping the sweat from pouring down my back.

I look out beyond the trees to see the clear blue ocean pushing up to the edge of the horizon. I am filled with gratitude. I did it. I live my dream life sitting in a treehouse in paradise. I sit here now because I let go. Life is so fucking good because I found the light within myself and found a way to start sharing it with the world. I let go of the need to control anything that comes my way because I know it is in my best interest. Amor fati- loving one's fate. I have fallen in love with my destiny because I surrendered. I put all my trust into the guidance being placed in front of me. I found the clues, solved part of the puzzle. I share my story because the time is now. This journey is not easy, and I am not here to tell anyone that it is. In this book I will share with you my journey and lessons I learned along the way. I will give you guidance where I felt helpless. I will give you strength in understanding. My journey will not be the same as anyone else, but the feelings might be. Even when you feel alone you never are truly alone. I never had any interest at all in writing a book before. Not one bit. But then my life became a fairy tale. I followed my dreams. My intuition. The idea that I loved which was traveling the world. I had this uncanny desire to experience the earth fully and completely. Not knowing how that could ever be satisfied until my adventure on a sacred island in the middle of the ocean. I felt ragingly inspired to get this book going when I opened my manifestation journal for the day. I did not have much to write, which was quite unusual for me. I would fill pages upon pages the second I got the thing in my hands. I never stopped writing whatever thought I was thinking. But this day, I had nothing. So, I flipped through the pages thumbing for something inspiring when I found myself at the very beginning. "There is no remedy for love but to love more." Henry David Thoreau. A quote from an Urban Outfitters fortune cookie booklet which I had taped in the opening page. It had no real reason for being there. I grabbed one of the quotes then stuck it to the beginning because I thought that was what other people did in their journals. As I gazed upon the quote, it hit me. The real connection as to why I did put it there a month ago, to serve me in this present moment. At the time, it meant nothing other than a way to start my journaling process. But in that moment sitting in the hot summer heat I began to feel the love Thoreau was talking about. The giving kind of love. When we feel full of love everything in the world feels possible. The more love we put out into the world the more it can be felt around us. The more love we extend in even the smallest of details, the more it consumes us and grips us tight. The more love we give the more we receive but the idea is not to expect love because we receive. Our ego stands in the way of true love for true love is nothing at all because we must expect nothing in return. We should love because we want to feel nothing and everything at the same time. We should not give because we expect but give because we love. Love is limitless because it renounces all of its limits. Love loves to love, LOVE! It was in this moment that I wrote: Thank you ADHD for scattering my brain across the surface of thought, space and time. One thought leads to another and before I know it, I am way too far ahead of myself to catch up to the previous thought I was having. Lists upon lists upon lists that were always started and never finished. They say we have up to 60,000 thoughts per day, maybe more. And I know we all can think thoughts, but some of us have more organized filing cabinets than others. My thoughts were always hard to keep track of. Thousands of random inspirations that would never reveal themselves in physical form. Remaining fleeting thoughts lost in the void of non-completeness. Even the times that I would make the effort by inserting them in a note on my phone, they would become buried and non-remembered. That is why I started journaling. Writing down any thought, idea, memory, or moment that would appear in my head. I wanted to remember and reflect as much as I possibly could. I wanted to connect the dots. So, I did, and this story tells my constellations. The constellations of my life. This book is my commitment to myself and to all the fleeting thoughts that had yet to reveal themselves in a finished project. Jack of all trades, master of finally one. I put so much love into these pages. I poured so much soul, this book is my muse. These pages are filled with some of the happiest times of my life thus far. It is my intention that whoever picks up this book feels the light that runs through the black ink printed here. I want you to touch adventure and breathe discomfort. This is a life meant to be lived and a lot of us spend our time as slaves. Be as wild and creative as the inner child that runs trapped and lost within. Then one day you find her, him, or them and realize that growing up was a distraction.

II

Breathing into the Self

E VERY SINGLE TIME we are filled with an abundance of thought we are filled with the divine intelligence, the collective consciousness that bridges us all as one. I used to think I was a magician when I would get high with my high school friends. Thoughts would stream into my head from what felt like nowhere. "High thoughts are the best thoughts." We used to say. There is a reason for that. Do we even know that the voice in our head is the voice that always speaks? Where do the voices in our head come from and where do they go? I am not sure that any of us really know, even when we think we know. The collective conscious that connects us all is being pinched. We live in a world so disconnected and not because we are forced into quarantining away from each other, hidden behind masks and social distancing. We are disconnected from our spiritual selves and in turn are disconnected from one another. Life's not supposed to be so serious, it's an experience. Its love, and laughter. Full of life! We are all walking our own path, sometimes crossing and connecting with others. When I first started on the path to a more enlightened spiritual life I felt as though I was teetering around a little out of balance with myself and out of alignment with my path. Until some words were brought into my life from a magical friend named Katie. Her mysteriously dark features held space for healing, and space for guessing. The moment I met her I was drawn right to her eyes. Locked in a calming glance we shared a hug. We had only just met, but it felt like I knew her for a lifetime. I never had anyone hug me like that. An embrace filled with time and purposeful breathing. Breathing is something that we all take for granted. It happens so naturally we barely notice it is there sometimes. When we are reminded and asked to take notice so many parts outside of the breath seem to disappear. We might stop hearing the dogs barking, or the sound of cars driving past the street. Breathe is the focus center of our body. Breathing is natural and essential to life. But so many of us aren't practicing. It is the first and last step we take in life yet so many of us aren't feeling its strength. Breathe does not have to be an unconscious behavior. So much of what we do is unnoticed until we wake up to our spiritual self. Waking up is the process of realizing we are one small microcosm in the macro. Before I woke up, I went through life on autopilot. Completely unaware of what I could be aware of. It was like I was eating food without even tasting. Stomping through life without considering how abrasive so many parts of myself were to not only me as an individual but to others around me. As we wake up, we become more aware of those that surround us, including the thoughts surrounding our conscious mind. In learning to be conscious of these things, we can realize how subtle all the movement throughout our body feels.

The breath. Take a breath. As you take the breathe read these words slowly so as to soak up a new bit of oxygen with each letter streaming across the page and as you get to the point of which you can no longer suck in any air. Sit still. Sit still with the air that has filled your lungs and empty it out. Feel the relaxation float across the organs inside of you as much as the skin outside of you.

As we learn to master our breathe, we learn to feel our bodies. We can feel the subtle heartbeat that jumps if we hold our breath too long. The more oxygen we can receive, even into the smallest of our cells, the stronger we become. Tuning into the ability to be fully conscious of every breathe and action we take with each present moment that passes is awakening. Tuning in to the conscious mind is as easy as flipping on the switch of a lightbulb. If, you are open to it. It is a miraculous thing to be able to have self-reflection. To reflect on our actions as a human being. Take a moment and reflect on the breath. In through the nose, and out through the mouth. Sigh. Let it out.

Take another one. A breath with gratitude. Gratitude for the weight that our body must hold in order for us to keep going.

Our body that graciously never asks for thanks but keeps working. A body that continues breathing even when we stop noticing that it is there. This time take another nice breath. Some of you might have skipped over the first few breathes thinking it was unimportant. The old me would have. But take this moment, on this page and hold the book into your hands. Breathe into the grass or couch, beach or hammock. Wherever it is that you reside as you read my words. A simple breath. In through the nose and out through the mouth. Count for five in, and out for five. Repeat this for as long as you feel called. I hope that you find peace for a moment. Bliss comes not from ignorance but from patience. Be patient with yourself and my words. There is no rush to finish. So, sit with yourself and breathe. When you find yourself here at these words, smile. You believe it or not, just meditated. Maybe, at this point, you want to set the book down and maybe you want to keep reading. But let this be a moment where you can sit still with yourself. If you still skipped over the breathing and decided to keep reading take a moment first and be present with this page. With the present moment.

The start is never the beginning

When I first set foot on the spiritual train I fell off. Well, I jumped off into the forest chasing a life full of distractions only to find that I was starving myself. Mastering the art of distraction is one tough act to follow. There are always going to be distractions, better things to do, more 'important' things to do. Making time for ourselves and tuning in to our own energy is, in my opinion, the single most important thing that we can learn for today, tomorrow and yesterday. No matter how busy life gets, always dedicating time and space for ourselves. Covid-19 sure did shock the world, but it showed a lot of us that maybe some alone time is exactly what we need. A BREAK! Some space. A forced pause from the distractions. Time to the self is magical if we know how to do it right. I used to spend my time alone looking at the mirror disliking what I was looking at instead of going out and doing something about it. I used to spend my time alone distracted by social media instead of sitting... alone. Being alone is hard. Even when we are alone, we often find a way to distract ourselves from our self. The fear of facing the feeling of truly being alone. I no longer fear solitude because that is where I found myself a home. Being alone helps us to find the space within to feel love for our self. Feeling love within, is a building block to loving others. Love within our self is the highest and most valiant act of understanding. We grow past fear when we love the self. Spirituality is silly because we always have a choice. We call that choice freewill. Some people stumble upon the path of spirituality, stumble upon spirit and still decide to ignore it by filling up their lives with distractions. The first few times I stumbled onto the path I found myself nestled in the net of distraction. Tangled trying to get up with no seemingly sensible way out except through so I plunged my roots farther into the deepest centers of the planet. I committed to my habits making them permanent to prove to myself there was no such thing as resurfacing. The gas was lit inside of me and I was never going to be able to tame the flames again. Much like the earth's core full of molten lava, I felt the hot and burning desire to change myself and be a part of something bigger. Choosing to believe in the unbelievable. Breathing in the wonders of this mystical plane. The words that my magical friend Katie said were simple, "darling you were never off the path." Despite embarking on the journey and running away from it several times the lessons I learned were necessary to bring me exactly where I was in that moment with her. Divine order they say. It is always part of the plan. My life almost flashed before my eyes in a wave of harmonious action. In that moment I realized that my story would never have unfolded in the beautiful way that it did had I not stumbled off and on again. Through all the triumphs and the tribulations. If I had been anyone else, if I had chosen to live or do anything else in my life it would never have been exactly as it was. The journey is not linear, it is a constant circle bringing you round and round. For me the round and round went around a lot quicker because history does in fact repeat itself, unless we learn the lessons, we are supposed to learn the first time around. It took me a few circles to get it right.

Choosing University

Life was normal before I woke up. I went to high school in a really small town in Central Pennsylvania. A town where rolling green hills, endless cornfields and open meadowy landscapes meets growing suburbia. Where a night out on the town was spent popping into the local gas station just to see all your friends, sit in the booth and catch up on whatever local drama was circulating the loop. I wasn't really anything special, I did all the normal things. I threw parties at my parents' house when nobody was home, the best parties until I got caught. I played sports. I was well-liked. Popular, I guess you could say. But it was only because I was such a people pleaser and tried way too hard to make everyone else happy. I never spoke up for myself and was truly deep down, super insecure. I had friends and did life the way everyone else did. Got into trouble, had some fun, and continued down the path which led me to comfortability. Normality. I was always a happy kid, but I was truly not myself. I was so cautious and overly judgmental of myself. I was damn sure good at being a sham. Smiley Abbey, always happy. I was always battling something. My parents divorce took over the better half of my childhood. So there was always usually some sort of drama at home. People in high school can be so judgmental and I always took everything to heart. People were always so immature, especially about sex. Someone had found out that I lost my virginity and wound up spray painting my name underneath the bridge close to my house where dozens of people could see. It was so embarrassing to get bullied for being open to an experience as a woman. I always got picked on for being a whore. Which really used to irritate me. I compared myself to everyone and never really did too well in front of the mirror. Constantly wondering why I look this way when there are so many other beautiful women I thought to be better than me. The great thing about sports was that it allowed me to channel my energy into something real. I always had natural talent as an athlete. When I decided to go to college, I only applied to one school that I had no doubt I would get accepted to. A small university in the North East corner of Pennsylvania called East Stroudsburg great for their division II sports and even better at being in the middle of nowhere. Pennsyl-tuckey we called it. It wasn't necessarily like I thought that I had it all figured out when I made the decision, but I was way too stubborn to turn my back on my commitment. Signed on the dotted line of a piece of paper was my promise to attend this university to play lacrosse there on scholarship. In high school I was either at practice for one of the two sports I played, playing on my club team, at personal training, running to get better and faster, or just shooting around by myself. I worked so hard at it and desired to keep getting better. Lacrosse was my life, so I wanted that part of my life to continue. Sports were the only thing that I did outside of school.

I had several offers from colleges, but I chose this one because of a strong connection I had with the coach and the atmosphere. My first visit was spent with welcome arms. It was not the craziest party scene; it was a small upgrade from the high school parties I used to throw. What brought me in wasn't the partying and it wasn't the college itself, it was the family that I saw on the team. All the girls were extremely passionate about playing the game and united together as a real family. The university did not have the best of facilities but that was not what mattered to me. I was inspired by the love and laughter that all the girls shared, and the talent that was on the team. I truly didn't even bother looking at any other schools. I refused to tour because I was following what I thought

I wanted for myself, even though I had absolutely no direction in a career whatsoever. Choosing this school was easy, I couldn't fail. I didn't even have to submit my SAT's. Part of me was also scared of disappointing my dad. He was always there at every game I had ever played, took me to all my far club tournaments, supported me, coached me…He was ecstatic to see me continue as an athlete into college. Being an athlete felt like it was the only thing I knew how to do well. I pursued sports and quit almost every other talent I had in my life. The athletic life swallowed me whole, I quit my artistic self- passions. I had no direction, no real drive to have a certain career. My loss of direction leads me to go to school for business. My dad was successful in business so I thought that I could do the same. I got accepted to East Stroudsburg early from the deal I had with lacrosse and made my plans to finish out high school. Senior season was to go according to that idea of a plan, then graduation, then finally I would go to play the sport for one of the top ten teams for division two lacrosse. But life loves to show us that nothing ever goes according to plan. The utter disappointment and shock as I fell 8 goals away from my 100th was gut wrenching. I'm a petit girl and would get tossed around a bit almost every game at least once. It's an intimate contact sport and I was always near all the action. This time, 8 goals short, I really couldn't get up. No help to the bench for the stubborn girl I was. It was over, I knew I broke it. It was extremely painful, but my dad and I agreed to just shake it off, so I went to school the next day avoiding the issue only to realize that at one point I could not walk anymore. I hoped it wasn't true but as we went to the doctor, they told me that I would be in a boot for a possible three months. It was right before my 18th birthday and prom. I fractured the tiniest little bone in my left foot that is basically impossible to break. Sesamoid bones in the foot are difficult to treat because of the location and surrounding tissues. It was painful having to watch the rest of my senior friends play out the rest of the season without me. Reflecting on that moment I was probably meant to break my foot and avoid East Stroudsburg, but I did not know that it was a signal to listen. What I failed to recognize at the time was that I needed to slow down. I was so naive and stubborn. This was the first sign, but I did not know to perceive it as such at the time. I asked why me? Why now? My mom was right. There always comes a time when we realize just how right moms are and I am the last person to want to bring up this cliché. My mom questioned my decision to choose East Stroudsburg but I was way too stubborn to listen to her inquisition. I did not stop and listen when I broke my foot, when I was first asked to slow down and avoid the distraction. I chose the safe route. The easy way. Going to college for the first time IS exciting no matter where you end up going and I was excited to get out of my parent's grip. Even more to get out of my small town. At this school I was playing for one of the most competitive divisions in the entire nation. I was partying hard and playing harder than I had ever done before. It was a challenge and I never backed down from competition. I wanted to be the best! But after a few weeks, I began losing my sense of connection to the place.

Mostly because of the people I was surrounded by. I did not feel the sense of family I felt when I came to visit. I did not feel truly loved like other people had made me feel in my life. It did not feel like home. I struggled for a long time to grapple with the way college was going for me. I had come back so strong and resilient after breaking my foot, but nothing seemed to be working out. And it was because I did not belong. The harder I tried to fit in the worse I felt. I cried myself to sleep every night wondering what was wrong about me. I did not want to admit that I might have been depressed because I was so good at pretending that everything was always okay, when it really wasn't. Not one bit. It wasn't that I was not liked, I was amiable with everyone on the team. Everything appeared great on the surface, I wore a smile on my face every day. But it never changed the way that I was feeling inside. Even though I was not diagnosed with depression, I certainly was mentally unwell. I was struggling but I passed my feelings off as irrelevant. I had it so good. I was supported and loved by my family, privileged enough to get to go to school in the first place. I had food on the table and did not have to worry about my survival. I used to think I could never feel depressed. I blocked everything out and continued pretending. Feeling so judged and overly empathetic to people who wanted nothing to do with me or my personality. Feeling so outcasted by being my own self. Feeling like no part of me was ever going to be truly happy. Feel a true belonging anywhere. It was a repeat of high school. Pretending that everything was okay. It was then, in those moments that I realized I would have rather been alone than feel lonely amid any group which I did not belong. Had I fit in; I never would have kept going. Kept reaching for whatever I always felt was out there waiting for me. I was unhappy and struggling. So, I changed it. I found a way to escape by studying abroad. I knew I wanted to travel, and this was the fastest way of making that happen. If it was for school, it was important so my parents were sure to help me figure that out. The plans were made and I couldn't get out fast enough. Even though I still enjoyed the ride. We sure were top ten. We were winning games and traveling all over the state. We were so successful in the season that we went to the NCAA final four tournament in Florida. A moment that I will never forget. Choosing ESU was never a mistake. It was not a failure. I now know that there is no such thing as failure only lessons in life on earth. I value so much of what lacrosse had taught me. I value not fitting in and all the mental struggles I battled every night and day putting on a mask acting like everything was okay. It made me tough, mentally tough. College sports taught me everything about pushing the body past its limits. When I struggled to cope with being a castaway, I remembered my strength. Knowing that I could push my body every single day to the max because that is what I did at practice. Out-hustle myself out of shear mental breakthroughs despite my sore body telling me "no!" We can push ourselves about 50% more than what we already think is our breaking point. The ceiling is a lot easier to break than one might think. I learned what I always needed to learn while I was there. I value the choice I made; I do not regret it. Failure, by lesson is strength. We all struggle when it comes to the fork in the road. If I go left, I get this, right I get that. Now I reflect and wonder if I could have understood the messages better, the signs that were always there and made a better decision. But I was completely unaware of how guided I always was, until I woke up. When it comes to making decisions, we do not have to make them alone. The guidance we seek is there if we know how to listen. And it helps in making the best ones. We can ask and when we learn how to listen, then we shall receive. Asking the universe for advice is a comical game. No question is too big or too small to get answered, but it all happens in divine timing. Sometimes the answer is immediate while others it takes time. The better we are at asking the right questions the more accurate the answer will always be. Even when some of the experiences that make me who I am today were not the best decisions I know it happened the way that it did for a greater purpose that I currently fulfill. Sure, the universe might have tried to warn me when I broke my foot, that going to play lacrosse was not in the highest of interest for me. But one of the many crazy things about humans on earth is our capability of free-will. At that time in my life I did not think TO think about the meaning in anything happening to me, it simply happened. But now, I know from every corner of my being that there is no such thing as a coincidence. It all happens as it should in alignment with a higher purpose. One day, it all too easily just makes sense.

III

Evolving the Self

HEN I LEFT for my study abroad experience in my sophomore year of college, I knew that it was going to be filled with moments exactly like I had imagined. I was dreaming of escaping my miserable time at school and my extravagant life abroad. "Isn't that in Germany?" Almost everyone that I knew from my small hometown had no idea that Belgium was even a country. Small town minds I suppose. I find that people who do not step out of their comfort zones, or expand their horizons become stuck in the ideas that they form around themselves. They create a box. In that box contains all their ideas about the world from what they see in media or hear from stories. The whole world might seem like a box for them because they haven't ever experienced it. Yes, Belgium is its own country, it is not in Germany. Brussels chose me, I applied to a ton of different programs but the one in Belgium was the only one that accepted me. One month in and I found myself loving who I was again. I made some of my best friends from all over the world, ate some of the most fantastic food, expanded my experience with a whole new language, new culture, and gained the best 25lbs I ever gained. I was learning so much from my experiences traveling abroad, especially when my phone got stolen. I got a little too drunk one night at the bar and completely lost track of everything I had with me. Pickpocketing is real, and it happened to me. I was forced to live life without a phone for about a month until my cheap replacement could come. So, I started reading this book that was brought to my attention. Sapiens by Yuval Noah Harari. Traveling helps us gain perspective and get out of our comfort zones. When we travel, we are brought to new ideas expanding reality itself. My small-town mind was growing, expanding, evolving. A seed was planted with Harari's mind- blowing concepts. Evolving? What could that possibly mean? I thought we already went through that. Or at least what I had come to understand in high school was that we were evolved far beyond our ancestors in the past. I was raised to believe the present moment is as advanced as we will be, and the science that came before us is the best science there is.... no. The greatest thing about evolution is that it is a never-ending revolving door. New science replaces old science, as well as new ideas and ways of thinking about understanding the world. Computers are far more intelligent than we think they are. Metadata is collected and put in collections of profiles that know more about us than we might know about us. Google and Facebook are not SKYNET, but they have an immense amount of power over society that needs protecting. It holds our individualities, our identity. Information is no longer tangible; it is communicative instruction. Artificial intelligence and genetic engineering are at the forefront of the Anthropocene. The abundance and access of data have permitted for easy connections all over the world. Connected by the ability to exchange information. With that information we are able to answer more questions.

We can combine various schools of thought within seconds by

using algorithms to pull out the most important information. That saves a lot of human time and resources. Information is represented with a deliberate purpose. It is all structured in feedback loops that keep us thinking the way that we do. It keeps us separate. That separation is the result of the abundance of globalized 'connection' we have. We are instantly connected, instantly checking, updating, loading more and more until we can't. We are glued into the algorithm itself. Stuck in the feedback loop and disconnected from reality. What is reality? The trees. The birds, and the sky. The earth! Waking up spiritually is the process of loving awareness. Awareness is the next step in the evolutionary chain, not the mergence with technology. As one evolves so does another. As we continue to advance and evolve, I find it important to note what is amazing about living in the 21st century is the abundance of knowledge we are collecting all over the world every day. Every second, because of technology. Modern science is catching up with ancient knowledge. Knowledge that has been harassed and pushed out of every indigenous or ancient society. It has been cast out as savage. Stigmatized as primal unintelligent discovery. Ancient knowledge and religious texts predicted our current end-of-the world 'apocalypse'. Even though the end of the world for most people has entailed toilet paper shortages and loss of WIFI connection. Ancient knowledge about spirituality and discovering one's intelligence. The ultimate truth which is still being hidden from the majority of society. Part of that truth lies within the story I tell here, my truth. My truth in understanding our divine connection to spirit. In understanding the sharing of ancient knowledge getting us where we are today. The life our ancestors' built for us. We are evolving, and to say that this is the best that is yet to come would be ludicrous. I am not quite sure why so many people believe that the way that we think is any better than the knowledge that came before us. We buy into ideas in the same way humankind always has. Capitalism, nationalism, consumerism, Buddhism even veganism are all IDEAS. The concept of abiding by rules because something or someone says so is exactly what we continue to do. The Greek's worshipped polytheistic Gods. They worshipped them and bowed to their belief systems which told them how to behave and what to do. The early founders of America came up with a set of beliefs which we simply have abided by for centuries. The ism's of the world are replacement God's. These ideas confine what we believe. We are simply agreeing to an economic, socio-political ideology that narrows our creative thinking. The God's we follow today are broken and we are realizing that being human is an imperfect process! We can no longer strive for perfectionISM because we must fail. Why are we so afraid of failing? Of trying anything new? Challenging the belief systems that tell us how we should live our lives. As if all the ism's we abide by are the best and only the best ideas we will ever have.

Change is the only thing that is constant and as far as survival goes, only the ones who adapt to change live on. We have come a long way since the pyramids of Egypt, but we are no better or farther ahead in human history than them. We use brick instead of stone and are still as vulnerable to disease and illness if not more now than some of our ancestors. What have we lost? Gained? When you break it all down, we are the same. Humanity is always humanity and life is always going to be imperfectly divine. It's a beautiful time to be alive because we get to witness this transitional point in human history. I used to condemn the idea of new technology because it was hurting our way of natural being. But now I see exactly why it needed to happen this way. This is the turning point, without this sort of technological growth spirituality would have never been able to be 'proven' to this degree. Neuroscience, quantum physics, epigenetics, and so many more fields of science are evolving our level of understanding about the world we interact with. The world we as an individual experience and grow in. Spirituality is scientifically fact-based science. It can no longer be cast out as evil-witchcraft. As lunacy. The time and age of pure light is on the horizon. True universal goodness. The universe pushing humanity through another stage of evolution. A shift in the paradigm. Altering the consciousness of our brains. We have entered an even more expanded understanding of the earth. How it functions in the quantum realm, how we can interact with the realms. Humans reflect on the various revolutions that have occurred in the dynamic growth from apes to homo sapiens. Agrarian to industrial. This new cycle is the conscious age, 5D, post-human. We cannot be naïve enough to think that what we have now is the best that we can ever have. This IS evolution and with climate change as the pressing time clock on earth's survival it is about time everyone start to wake up. To wake up to the destruction of this planet. This is the next phase of evolution. The great awakening.

The level up which challenges all beliefs we ever held before about reality itself. When we start to ask the deepest questions about our limits. Could we use the technology we have today to make peace, not war? To heal the planet rather than blow her to pieces? Drying up all her seas? The way we use so much of the technology today is a waste on how exponentially limitless we are. Using social media as an ego stroke rather than a magical connecting button to the entire universe to get anything we could ever want. Connect with anyone we could ever want to connect with. I used to use technology so mindlessly until I woke up. Began to evolve. New ideas emerge every day. Who are going to be the ones who break through these old paradigms to birth new ideas into light? Survival of the fittest, only those who adapt to change are the ones that thrive on. Only those that wake up are those that are able to understand their conscious mind. A revolution is happening and the people who are going to shift the consciousness of the planet are the ones who quit wasting their time turning around reaching out their hands to those who are not ready to lift up their own weight. It's all part of the process of growing, and out-growing. Of evolving ourself and knowing that other people who are behind are going to have to run to try to catch up to those who are already flying. The momentum is picking up. I used to think that evolution was in history's past, when in fact it is happening still right now. Technology IS guiding us toward the consciousness shift, the level up we did not know we had in us. We are extraordinary beings, let's start to think extraordinary things! Eliminate limits, we are moving to the place beyond belief-isms. These isms give people something to share but it also creates a ceiling. Reach for the stars and reach even further. Imagine reaching for the light within that star. That same light that exists within the star belongs to all of us. All the time we reach we fail to realize what we reach for is already inside. The evolving process, revolving door, means we will open and close so many. We evolve and lose bits and pieces of ourselves that no longer serve the present us. Before waking up or evolving we live our lives in the mirror of distractions that exist on the physical plane. We look at cars and trees and birds. We have no reason to think that those things are anything but what we understand it to be. We can see it, sense it, smell it. But as we wake up, we question. We question the existence of a bird. What makes that a bird? Does everyone see this bird the way that I do? Why is this bird existing? Is it even a bird at all? Leveling up or evolving asks that we question our acceptance of ideas. A bird exists in front of us as we experience it. Experience is the physical 3D plane and everything we associate to normality. We see, touch, taste, smell, feel. But what about really seeing or really feeling? We see things with our eyes to a degree but what are we actually seeing? No sensory 3D experience is alike, we all experience our own individualistic realities at the same time we sit in the same room. Science tells us we flip images in our eyes upside down and right-side up to create the picture we understand that we see. Colors are frequency in the same as sound. Normally we are not seeing the sound, although that is possible with practice. Some people have synesthesia and hear or see colors. We hear with our ears but not everyone has the same level of hearing. Some have trained their ears beyond the physical 3D plane, and that is where we find mediums and psychics who tap into the frequencies beyond what we were raised to understand. We can be nose or taste blind in the same way that eyesight can be blind. Imagine if we were able to hone in on all of the sensory abilities we have and maximize the use we got out of all of them at once? Spirituality IS science. Spirituality is the part of our brains that we lost and why so many people are not evolving. Tapping into the spiritual parts of the brain connects us with the greater power above. The power we all are capable of when we think beyond our sensory experiences. Spirituality is waking up to the human experience itself. So many of us have been lying dormant for so many years.

We are capable of creating our own magic, we are destined for treasure on this earth. We were never meant to succumb to so many of the delusions we see in the reality we live today, the feedback loop. The structures that play a part in keeping us controlled, brainwashed. Waking up spiritually removes us from the screen and resets the loop. Helping to pull ourself out to watch as it spins and spins. When I realized I pulled my head out of the screen, and became the observer,

I noticed just how stuck everyone was. Marveled at the fact that i was trapped for so long until I found the beauty in walking away. The beauty in realizing that it wasn't about how long I was trapped but in the journey unfolding before me. My suffering, was over. My true and real suffering. As if I knew that the path was always supposed to happen in just this way. The moment I walked away from the feedback loop I opened up my world to love. To a forest of big tall trees. Trees that were grown from the seeds of my past. The seeds that I collected every step of the way from every book, every person that I met, every friendship that I ever had which brought me to exactly where I sit in the forest today. In this forest I wonder who decided to teach all of us that life doesn't have meaning? Who came up with the word coincidence? We are powerful beings, things do not happen out of coincidence. Life always has meaning. We are written out of the stars. We are made of stardust. It is in our DNA and if something as galactic as stardust is within us, then does that not make it entirely possible we are as far out as the galaxy we see? When we find meaning in life and connect all the right dots, fate aligns itself in perfect harmony so long as we listen. So long as we admire the puzzle that life presents in front of us. A true Sherlock Holmes in life. I believe people are too afraid of how powerful they might be and turn on themselves, or at least their ego does for them. They approach the fork in the road only to avoid it by turning around and going back to where they came from. Or they approach the fork and envision a wall to be climbed first. But the wall only exists because they built it themselves. They starve themselves of the love and light that awaits them by choosing the path of ignorance over presence. Hatred over gratitude. Anger rather than kindness. Fear over courage that it takes to climb the wall that they put up for themselves in the first place. It is our free will to choose to honor our purpose on earth or to run from it. To choose to be courageous we have to question the mind, open the heart, and dare to dive into our own destiny. Nothing is permanent and everything is always changing. We have the capability of changing our futures. It is not fate if we do not design it to be so. Indecisiveness is procrastination. Eventually everyone must walk this great path whether it occurs in this lifetime or the next. If we feel lost at the divergence of paths wondering which one is the right one, it's okay so long as we just choose. Something might have told us to pick the one on the right but we chose the one on the left where we got more lost and had to carve our own way out. Neither one of the roads is right and both of them create our life's stories. Choosing to go to school for lacrosse felt like it was the right thing to do, until it wasn't. But I learned, I was bumped and bruised inside and outside. When we make mistakes we miss-and-take the wrong path. Life never happens to us. It happens for us. It happens as it should and sure, I miss took a path but I learned, and grew stronger. Life is not perfect. Creation is perfect and created us imperfect to experience it all. Imperfection is completion. No matter how many times I edit out the contents of this book so much of what I learned might have already changed and it would almost be impossible to keep up! Always evolving and growing to oneness. To balance and the imperfectly perfect. Choosing to wake up pushes us to the realization that we never have to miss and take the wrong path ever again. We have to stop pushing them away. Procrastinating evolving. It's scary. Facing our feelings is scary. To have the power to do anything you could possibly dream is scary when all you know is what someone else always told you. But you are not alone. You are guided and loved by so many. Just because you cannot see it does not mean it is not there. You were born for a reason. Believe in that purpose and you will find true bliss.

IV

Universal Self

MANIFESTATION IS A term that I had become super aware and familiar with when I started working for this massive commercial seafood restaurant on the Jersey Shore. I had returned from Europe and finished out my time at East Stroudsburg, FINALLY. The next chapter of my life was off to a great start because I was moving in with my step mother to live beach side for the summer. 2019 summer. Money was everywhere and I was so irresponsible with it. I was making way more money than I knew how to handle and wasting it all at the bars, on clothes, and all of the unimportant materialistic things I enjoyed at the time. It was fresh and all of the people that surrounded me were fresher. It was one big party all day every day. Wake up, go to the beach, drink, go to work, drink some more then wake up and do it all again the next day. I made some amazing connections with the people I worked with there.

People who changed the trajectory of my entire life for the better.

I was trying to make photography my career because it would allow me the freedom to do whatever I wanted, and travel the world.

A true xenophile. I was going to use all that I learned about business and grow my very own photography one. I had the perfect controlled image of myself and what I was going to do. A great soul I met while working asked me to assist her in photographing a wedding. I was so excited to help out and get a jump start on my career. But life had a different plan, per usual. I was very poor at making time for myself because I was constantly keeping busy overworking 40+ hours a week to make all the cash that I could to be able to spend it when I went out with friends. Sometimes a little hammered to start the shift. It was the never-ending rocket going up, up, up until one day it all blew up in my face. It's hysterical, actually. I woke up in the middle of the night in agonizing pain. I never liked taking painkillers for aches and pains growing up. I would have rather suffered through it than take something to suppress the pain.

This pain was in the exact same spot where my fractured sesamoid bones were in the bottom of my left foot in high school. When a storm would come my foot would get irritated and act a little creaky. It was as if the broken part of my foot that had been disconnected from my body sought connection with the earth and brought some of the earth back into me as it healed, making my broken foot ache when a storm was on its way. This pain was not the creaky uncomfortable kind. It was hot and throbbing. I tossed and turned all night. Not even marijuana calmed the nerves. I went to urgent care first thing in the morning. I hobbled into the office to get someone to stop whatever was going on in my foot. After being admitted to the room, explaining my pain, they improperly assessed me and sliced my foot open to relieve some of the pressure thinking it was some sort of wart. I took an antibiotic and returned home feeling slightly relieved. I went to work thinking I would be fine and would just have to work through the pain. One hour into my shift and it was throbbing again but largely inflamed. I had to wait till the next day to get checked out by the doctor again. So, I laid in bed tossing and turning all night as my foot throbbed in pain. Broken. Broken again? I did not think that was possible for my foot to be broken again in the exact same place I fractured it two years before. It seemed impossible, I hadn't done anything to it. I fled for home to get a second opinion because I was in denial that one of my favorite summers would end with me in a boot. The swelling and throbbing pain continued on, but it did not feel broken. The doctor that I went to go see at home answered my prayers- my foot was not broken! But I did have an infection that was turning the inside of my foot purple. I was to remain off of my feet for at least a week, which was way better than the rest of my summer. I packed up my car toward my second home. Windows rolling down, music bumping as I cruised the country backroads instead of taking the highway my car broke down. First my foot, then my car. I was so caught up in the disasters I failed to remember that it was the same weekend that I was supposed to photograph the wedding. Everything felt like complete shit. Frustrated, forgetful, and nothing was going my way. I missed the career opportunity I thought would set up my future. My car was costing hundreds to fix and my foot was still in pain. Another week at home, away from my paradise life because the car was going to take a while. The day that I was leaving to go home I had my car packed for the shore when a giant bird flew into the window extremely aggressive. It hit the side about four times and really gave me a scare. I knew that was usually a symbol of a bad omen, but I let it go. Nothing was going to ruin my trip back after a two week hiatus. My friends missed me and my wallet was hungry. These were the last weeks of summer and I was going to live it up like I was before. So naturally, the minute I got back I threw on some platforms, jeans and took to the bars. My friends and I approached the bouncer with fake ID's. I went first, and it all happened too fast. He took the ID gave it to the cop and I was ticketed all within a five minute period. It did not matter how heavy I cried, they were sending me to court. I sat staring at the stars questioning why those things were happening to me, I looked up and the stars in the sky completely shifted. It was not a shooting star, the sky moved so I took a break from crying to check my phone. A text from my mother. The downward spiral was far from over. My grandmother just died. I had been meaning to visit her more that summer but by moving away it was easier to avoid. She had dementia and hadn't recognized me in years, but I felt so much guilt for not seeing her as much as I should have. It was hard to see her lose herself in a bed full of her own shit in the nursing home. She was always there for me and my sister when my parents were working. She was on hospice twice and recovered in the nursing home, she was truly so strong. Her spiritual presence became immediate in my life even though I was not entirely aware of it at the time. Life was not going right and summer was over. I wanted to try to make sense of everything that was happening to me, it wasn't 'just life'. Shitty things happen, but why do they happen? I sought advice on the internet and came across a podcast. One of the random interviews along the way wound up talking about luck. The woman in the interview said that there is no such thing as luck. Life is all about timing. By making ourselves available to opportunity at the right place and time. Then being adventurous enough to have the courage to ask and make shit happen. None of the events that transcribed were anything but results of the choices that I had made. There is no such thing as luck, good or bad in the same way there is no such thing as a coincidence. Things might not happen for a specific 'reason' but I do believe that it happens as it should. It happens because of a decision someone somewhere made. It happens because of a choice. Sometimes the choice is yours, and sometimes it is not. So many of the unfortunate events were incidences because of the choices that I was making, a clear sign from the universe to slow the fuck down. It was not bad luck. It was a sign. The podcast laid out ideas that never crossed my radar before. I was swallowed whole into a world of magic I didn't know existed. The word manifestation was brought up. Manifesting a desired future? Sure, I had ideas of goals as broad as daylight like having a family, traveling the world and being successful. The podcast made it clear that manifesting our future in detail is how we get what we want. 'in detail' was not part of my vocabulary. Possibly because it stressed me out to be too specific. I did not really know what I wanted, but I knew I wanted to travel the world and save it too. So I brought out the recording device on my phone and recorded myself for a week where I laid out some of my ideas about traveling the world. It felt good to start creating the life I wanted but, I was not understanding the principle correctly I was manifesting by wishing instead of actioning. Manifestation is part of a much longer process.

Manifestation is a lot harder without understanding oneness. The coexisting string that connects all beings on earth. We can wish all we want, but ultimately we must provide the action for it to reveal itself. There are a wide range of accepted laws that can be applied to the way that the universe actually works. It is not necessarily a belief system, but logic that helps us attain and understand things like karma. They are the natural wisdom. We can use the power of our minds to attract what we are. Like attracts like and the overarching understanding between so many of them is that every single thing on this earth is connected through energy which is relative to the idea that everything we say, do, and think affect the energy around us. A small part of the whole, a microcosm in the macro. All from the same source. Like I had touched on before, where all we experience is energy and vibration. Our actions are connected because the thoughts we make have their own vibrational frequencies. Like the law of attraction where what we think we attract. In manifesting something we can attract what we want but it is not that simple. We can't go out yelling at the world for saying, I want this then grow angry when we do not receive it. We become true manifestors when we become what we want. We act as though we have it and pursue a life that attracts what we are. If we think things, we attract them. If we act like those things we become them. We have to treat ourselves as if we are already what we want to become. Putting thoughts to words to actions, we grow and attract an abundance of what we desire. My dreams become a reality, but summer was coming to an end and all I could think about was parties. Parties to finish the summer, and parties that were on their way to me as I launched myself into the next phase of my life: Penn State. Riding high off of one of the best summers of my life, a true 'alchemist' so I thought. I dipped my toes in the water but failed to create a habit when I opened the doors to my next University. Still no actual clue what I was doing with my life. "The cult," never say never, because I had always said I would never attend PSU. I separated myself from the idea of ever wanting to go there because if there is anyone that knows Penn State, they're everywhere. I wanted to be different and going there was not an easy separation from everyone else I grew up with. But I was pleasantly surprised to find a home in the people I met right away. Real friendship. It barely took anytime at all to adjust and I was enjoying college for the first time. It was not a cult at all, it was one of the best universities in the nation with connections all over the world. Iwas enjoying the parties, again. I forgot about all the knowledge I was acquiring and stopped manifesting. I was getting drunk instead. I was doing college the way it should be done. I had football, friends, my boyfriend, my family and a great education. Penn State was never just a college decision, neither was my degree path in communications. It was fate. The professors I had and classes I took were all stepping stones perfectly laid out for me to cross. I might have forgot about manifesting my fantasies but found grounding information about reality. The truth in communication. The universe brought me to Penn State. To specific classes and professors who changed my entire outlook on life giving me an even broader scope to understanding the way that the world worked. How Disney movies inherently programmed fear and grief into our hearts as children. How marketing company's used and developed various tactics with science to physically addict us to their chemically juiced-up products. How manipulated we are in every meanderingly 'normal' thing about society. Even the city streets that we live and walk in, take the suburbs for example. Grid system suburban homes with plots of grass, houses that look the same, rows and columns of perfectly organized systems that keep us stuck in the feedback loop. A perfectly organized filing system of people in their homes obeying orders. Completely unaware of their transient state of 'perfect'. My lenses were magnified and I was reflecting on the world a whole lot differently than I ever had. This is when I began asking even deeper questions. What was going on? As aimless as my life felt I knew something was pushing me toward something great. Now, as I write these words I gaze at the clock at 2:22. A beautiful synchronicity proving to myself once more that my confusion and aimlessness was always for a reason. Always purposeful even at times when it felt hopeless. I knew I would be happy and successful no matter how many times people would ask me what my career would be. "Communications, what are you going to do with that?" I truly did not think that college was ever going to do anything for my career in life. I was always just figuring it out. More pieces to the puzzle in this crazy miracle we call life. Strolling along but still at the time, stuck in the loop. Thankfully I grew to acquire more knowledge but also managed to create my best college life. Best college life implied first spring break planning. The entire spring semester dragged on, all I could think about was my ultimate getaway with my best friends leading up to my 21st birthday. But, per usual life slapped me with a nice 2x4. The week leading up to the trip my world fell apart once again. It was one day before the trip and my boyfriend broke up with me. Riding that emotional roller coaster felt like enough of a heartache until I get a phone call hours later. My grandparents were married for 75 years and my grandfather had just passed away. Their love was the glue of the whole family and will forever symbolize so much more than that for me. 75 years is a long time to not only commit to someone else, but to never stop loving them. Their love for one another never burned out and it never will. I thought at the time that my boyfriend would be my 75 year love, so I lost a big piece of myself. My heart was sad. I felt the loss stream across my chest. My family would never be the same. My life would never be the same but spring break was one day away, I was not kissing this adventure goodbye.

V

Awakening Myself

WHEN THE PANDEMIC struck I was clubbing my life and dignity away on spring break in Barcelona. I was returning to a city that brought me some of my best partying memories and I couldn't wait to relive it. The drugs, the music, the drinking, the clubbing... All higher than high experiences for a soon to be twenty-one-year-old female. That same almost twenty-fun year old was emerging in a cosmic magical shift setting everything in motion. Before my awakening I never would have thought of the symbolism dealing with snakes to be correlated with anything positive. But leading up to the trip I was seeing snakes everywhere, it was too obvious not to notice. I had always associated snakes with evil thanks to my Christian background. Snakes represent rebirth and transformation which I thought to be perfectly fitting considering I was going through a break-up. I always wanted a spirit animal. Maybe the snake was my spirit guide carrying me through this personal growth and transition? One night we were walking through the middle of the city after a night of drinking when I heard a hissing sound. It was the most

35

bizarre thing to hear hissing noises come out of cobblestone paved roads, I thought for sure there was something magical going on. The next day we went to the market and I was looking for a new ring. I am normally extremely picky with rings, but this one took me not even thirty seconds to decide on. A silver serpent sitting right in the middle of the first glass covered box I laid my eyes on. A ring guardian that I could look upon every day to remind myself of my resilience. I was a snake shedding her skin. We carry on. We knew going into it that Covid-19 was wreaking its havoc in the Eastern part of the world, and most of Italy, but we had no fear. We really downplayed the whole thing, and our ideas were reinforced when no one seemed to be taking it seriously. There were no masks, no temperature checks, and no fear present from any of the people we spoke to about it. All my study abroad friends were being sent home in neighboring countries, but Spain was free and light-hearted. It practically didn't exist until Trump made the decision to close borders. I will never forget the fear-filled panic in my girlfriend's eyes as they called their moms and dads in despair attempting to get a flight home. I have never seen such a wild fight or flight response. Clothes were flying all over the apartment, tears were falling to the floor and screams were erupting out of pure desperation to get home to America while me and my other girlfriend, sat in a daze at what was unfolding. We couldn't help but smile at each other and laugh because not even an hour earlier did, we try opening a dialogue about the possibility of going home early, "gossip". We were shut down by their ignorance. Why would we dare ruin the mood by bringing up the Coronavirus? Why think that we might need to leave a few days early? Hours before even this discussion, and Trump's orders, my parents were up in arms overly worried about the intensity of the pandemic, which was what pressed us to talk about leaving early. We disregarded their advice too after all it was our spring-break, and we were too excited to be in another country. We were completely blinded to the reality of how severe it was. Lucky for us our parents' intuition made the right call by booking an early flight home for me and her so when the call was made about closing borders- we were safe with our flight leaving the next morning. Instagram and Snapchat flooded with videos of people scrambling from the club to the airport. I was sick to my stomach; I can remember feeling like my whole world was flipped upside down. This wasn't a big deal, right? Panic was everywhere in the air. At that moment I was sitting in our Airbnb pullout bed thinking how everything was about to change. One minute I was partying at the VIP section at one of the best clubs in Barcelona, the next I was being shipped back home to self-isolate in quarantine for two weeks. For the flight home my dad had made these makeshift masks with cloth and a rubber band attached with staples, it was so busted. The plane was full of spring-breakers desperate to get home. The airport was not orderly about explaining the situation, had everyone funnel into line that looked something like jamming Peter Griffin into an inner tube. Fear was in the atmosphere even in a plane thousands of feet up away from all the energy. When we landed, I immediately ran to check all my socials to see what was happening all over the world. Twitter was memed out, stock full of pandemic jokes and when I went to check my Instagram DM's. I had a message from a woman. A psychic in New York. She had come across an Instagram picture of mine on the explore page and saw my light radiating through my photo. "Your aura radius of red and gold. This transition you are about to emerge from is going to change your life. They told me to reach out to you." Auras are personal energy fields of light that radiate around us. They serve as a physical, mental, emotional and spiritual state of present being. The aura is a garment of light, like a cloak. Everything we do or think affects the flux of our energy, and so affects the aura. A strong and radiant aura resonates as full mind, body, spirit connection. When we honor and connect with all those parts of ourselves, we are fully able to be seen. Everyone can see aura if they practice. If someone has ever walked in the room and you have felt their vibe as if they were 'glowing' that is their aura! They're electromagnetic field. I sure was coming off a social high so maybe she was right. Maybe my aura was glowing, and I felt so special to have heard that my light was shining to a woman who had come across my post on Instagram. This psychic said that I would get closer to the universe than I had ever been before. It felt all too strange to have a random woman reach out to me on Instagram at the same time the spirit of the snake emerged. I sat in the car gazing at the familiar land that had raised me. It was terribly unsettling to feel the world sink into dark hues of grey while I felt so radiantly bright. "What did all of this mean?" I kept wondering. The symbols were everywhere but I did not fully understand. What was I transforming into? I hoped a butterfly of some sort. My transformation. My metamorphosis emerging from the silent muggy virus-stricken world. A slow haze of over-exhaustion fell over me as I sunk into the car. SNAP. I grounded in reality as the radio talk show host spoke Covid. I stopped letting my imagination take over. I forgot the rest of the world was turning cold. I remembered how powerful this moment was in history. Uncharted territory for everyone one earth. Maybe this weird feeling I was having was more outside-in than inside-out. The world was shut into lockdown. The transformation had nothing to do with me, it was the world being transformed. Disconnection sparked far worse than before as everyone began to live their lives behind a mask. Quite honestly the empty toilet paper aisles felt more terrifying than the empty streets.

Quarantine

To avoid the possible spread of the virus to my immune- compromised family I was shipped off to my apartment at school. When Penn State is absent of students, it's absent of the livelihood that keeps any sustenance to the place. While unpacking to an eerily quiet apartment full of dirt and dishes we had all left in the rush to get out for spring break I realized I would be completely alone for the next two weeks. I truly was not bothered. Why dwell on the fact that every single person in the world was supposed to be quarantining? No reason to have FOMO (fear of missing out) when nobody was doing anything. And, after a week of straight killing my insides, the quiet was well prescribed. Being entirely alone had its ups and downs. Time did not exist because there was nowhere to go and nothing to do. I got way far ahead on my school work for the rest of the semester, so I never 'had' to attend a zoom class. I made up my own routine. 8 am I'd wake up and make breakfast, then immediately order from my Uber Eats guy, Steve, because I was still hungry but too lazy to make more. 10 am cry about my ex - boyfriend. 12 pm dance around my apartment for the first time of the day, make more lunch. 3 pm think about the fact that I hadn't attended a single one of my zoom classes that day then attend the last one while putting my computer on mute to avoid the non-sense. 5 pm dinner, yoga, and more dancing and blasting music around my apartment. After about five days straight of doing this I needed a change, and in came Tik-Tok. As anyone in the 21st century knows, that app is a black hole. A void of endless content trapping your attention for hours. Feeding on the addiction of access and information. Pleasure and fun. It was my everything for the next day and a half I was dizzy by the time I got up to finally get food. I was extremely inspired by all of the creative content, and as a creator myself I thought I could live up to the hype. I tried, and failed a decent amount.

The more I started to dive into the content on the app the closer I got to unveiling information that I had never come across before. Strange connections were happening across vast pools that seemed like more than a coincidence. I always had a hunch my WHOLE LIFE, that everything in the world was connected who would have thought I was right. People always thought I was crazy. I would try to conceptualize everything I learned in school about evolution, history, religion. Where did it all intersect? I knew it had to be somewhere. I did not know where that somewhere was until the app presented something called a spiritual awakening at my door. I was skeptical because I grew up Christian but disliked everything about it. It didn't feel like the whole truth and I saw what Christianity did to other cultures in life. No God would ever inspire such horrifying behavior out of individuals. I saw what so many organized religions sought to impose upon people, control. Separation. A who's better? Spiritually speaking as above so below. There is not better only the same broken down into smaller and smaller bits. Like coconut shavings. Coconuts (humanity as a whole) offer so much to the world. The coconut meat by itself is shaped like the surrounding circle of the husk. It holds the shape of a perfect circle. It's white creamy sweetness fills the palate and quenches thirst. Shredding the coconut meat into flakes creates tons of different decadent pieces. The tinier the pieces the more extravagant the flavor. The whole coconut would never taste the same as all of the tinier pieces. The individual pieces are small and easier to taste. Humans are the small pieces. We are all small sweet coconut shavings that were once part of the whole coconut. But the tinier and more individual the piece the more the flavor. We all have our own flavor, but come from the same source. We are all souls connected to the same coconut. This concept umbrellaed over all the belief systems that I had ever come to acquire. This was bigger than religion. This was the intersection of life. The light sort of just turned on and that was when shittt started getting interesting. Manifesting became a daily practice in my life. I tried the 369 method. The upside down method. The speaking into your phone method. The "I want this" method, which truly didn't work out, I just had absolutely no idea of how it all worked. I was super interested in getting out of it what I wanted and when it was not happening I grew frustrated and practically tossed the idea out the window. Still, I tried to make This was the real transformation. It's amazing what alone time and self-reflection can do to someone. Two weeks of self-isolation later and I finally could return home to my family to do the exact same thing that I had been doing alone. Meditating. My twenty-first birthday was right around the corner. My initiation. I always used to hate it when my mom would tell me I could not party in HS, it was almost as if I knew that I would not be partying forever she would say "you are only (insert illegal drinking age here) you will have your whole life to party after you turn 21" But I did not care. I just wanted to have fun while I still could and thank god I didn't listen to my parents and got all of the partying out of my system before I turned 21 or else I would still be losing myself in the party scene. At this point I had been there done that early enough to know it was not going to continue to be a part of my life. Being around friends who were happy was the fun part, and sometimes I felt like it took alcohol for everyone to get to the point that I normally was always at. That isn't to say I did not enjoy drinking or partying but I craved the energy not the alcohol. I felt no need to go crazy in losing my inhibitions at twenty-fun. Instead I began playing games with the universe. Asking silly questions and recalling my ideas on manifesting I tried to create my future reality. I tried meditating and practicing yoga, developing a better sense of whatever I was learning. I tried applying it to my life and was not truly feeling its affects. However I heard about astral projection for the first time and squinted my eyes hard shut so long they grew red. I wanted to see cool shit and was determined to keep trying. I thought if the universe really was real then why not test it? So I brought out my magic 8 ball and began to shake. I started shaking and asking super vague questions about my future but every time it gave me the "cannot predict now". So I understood then right off the bat that it was a game. I always liked games so I figured why not put my two cents in to play. following a pretty good routine during quarantine. This was changing me, meditation was changing me. I always thought that I could never really meditate. Meditating was too hard for me, my scattered brain thought too much too fast. But that was just it! The point of meditation is not to push everything out. They say empty your mind. But all I could ever seem to do was fill it up. By allowing the thoughts to stream in. By focusing on them we can work through the thoughts. It is way easier to melt cheese by shredding it down than by putting in the whole cube. By allowing the thoughts to streamline across like subtitles to a movie we can realize our role to play as the observer...The questioner of those thoughts. By meditating often we can start to notice the patterns of what brings us to feeling sad or frustrated just as much as feeling joyful, or surprised. Meditation has no confined constraints, sure there are plenty of different meditation practices but it is not a one size fits all especially if it is something new. Sports and exercise are a form of meditation. Cooking and art are a form of meditation. We can meditate anywhere anytime, even if that means you decide you want to do it as you sit on the toilet. Sure, sitting Indian style, palms facing up, spinal cord stretched aligning the space between the universe and the earth through our chakra system is a great way to meditate...But it does not have to be so rigid. Lay down, get comfortable in your bed, in your favorite chair, sit in a swing, float in the ocean, stand up, do it before bed, do it when you wake up, do it in the middle of your evening run. Mediation is learning to be still with ourselves. Meditation IS mindfulness. Meditation is observation. If we sit and empty our minds completely we never face what is bothering us. We never question why, or bother understanding the reasons behind the emotions we have. Through meditation we learn to be present with ourselves and with the thoughts that fly into our mind. By allowing those thoughts to filter through, just as coffee drips into the container, we get stronger and stronger. The more we filter the thoughts for exactly as they are, the less power they have over us. The more potent we become. We are not our thoughts, we are not controlled by the thoughts we have. We can decide to do whatever we want with the thoughts that we have. We can erase them and forget them or remember them if we want to.

The voice in our head is not what controls what we do, we control what we do and sometimes we allow our thoughts to create what we say or do. But how often do we think something and say/do EXACTLY how we thought of doing it the first time. Thoughts can lead to actions, but when our actions equal our thoughts it becomes a plan. Power over ourselves comes from drawing the line between thoughts and actions. Meditation is a state of conscious awareness that provides direct access to the spiritual multiverse. The reason we sometimes do sit like

Buddha is because information can be shared through the crown down to the root of our spine into the earth connecting the spheres using us a conductors of that energy exchange. Imagine trying to shoot an arrow into a moving target? Possible, and works for some people. But a still target is like a still mind.

Easier to tap into. How did my meditation practice evolve? Well I chose to draw the line and observe the thoughts that went across the screen. I questioned those thoughts. I began observing my thoughts as characters in a movie. When we watch a movie we are watching characters develop personalities. Some personalities we question more than others. Some we relate to. We predict what those characters will do based off of those personalities. We grow suspicious of the characters that demonstrate certain parts of themselves that seem questionable, why can we not apply that same logic to the way we think about our thoughts? Let's say the character of this movie never goes on any dates, and eats nothing but ice-cream all of the time with their five cats. Without questioning or observing the character (thought) for all that it is we assume that they are lonely. If we look beyond what we see (experience/think) we reveal that the character is actually super in love with chocolate ice-cream and does not see value in being in a relationship. We have the capability to question the circumstances that reveal themselves to us but most of the time we sit and allow things to be what we see. We MUST question the reality we portray in our own heads and observe the thoughts for what they are. We must question those thoughts we have to gain insight to understanding why we have those thoughts in the first place. We have to dig and dig and dig until we find the root. Some roots, just like plants, are hard to get out. There are trees that grow hundreds of feet and would never come out of the ground with a machine. Then there are succulents that barely need a tug. Our thoughts are the same. How can we begin to observe our thoughts? By sitting still, and breathing. We can allow the ideas that pop into our heads to come in. When certain people or places, stressors filter through we can ask why? What purpose do these thoughts have in my head? Do I want them there? Are they thoughts? Or are they problems I need to work through? It can be difficult to find the right questions to ask ourselves especially when we might not have the right ability to understand the emotions that we feel. There are so many remedies available today to help with understanding the emotions and broadening our understanding beyond happiness and sadness. Happy and sad are umbrella terms filled with hundreds of more specific ones. Expand on happiness. Do we feel gratefully happy? Joyfully happy? Silly happy? Or do we feel morbidly sad? heartbrokenly sad? There are so many emotions to experience beyond those umbrella terms that we use. We are more than angry, sad, jealous, and happy. Learning the vocabulary is part of expanding our being. The more vocabulary we learn about emotions the better understanding we can apply to our livelihood. As I began meditating more regularly, I would close my eyes I began seeing shapes. I would almost have to squint with my eyes shut to make sense of the shapes I was seeing but eventually it became clear enough that I started to make out certain symbols and numbers that I had never seen before. So naturally I tried Google, "Square, triangle, with circle in middle." The symbols that came up were far from the ones that I was seeing in my head but when I tried to draw each symbol it was like somebody replaced the Mona Lisa with a stick figure drawing. Since I was completely unsure of what the symbols were it seemed unproductive to look into at the time when there were many more things to focus on. I stuck to what I did know how to understand: numbers. I would close my eyes and twist them shut throwing on my zoom as best as I could trying not to squint so the message would come through clearer. The colors ranged from a space green to a knightly purple. Sometimes they would show up red. They were never there for long. The numbers would fly at me in a mist and the sequences all made complete sense, once I googled them. It was fun, I was playing a puzzle with the universe or making it up myself. But either way, it made perfect sense. 9111 was the first sequence. The first search answer was a bible verse. Psalm 91:11 For he will command his angels conceding you to guard you in all your ways. Angels, my grandparents? Maybe it was and it made me feel safe. The next sequence, a message. Angel numbers were something that I had never heard of before. Angel numbers are one of the ways that our guides communicate with us in our daily lives. They are codes that give advice, and share messages that we may not fully understand for ourselves. Angels are messengers that carry divine vibrations for us to discover on earth. When the angels want our attention they will let us know. There are so many different possible combinations of numbers, and sometimes the expressions have specific meanings. Synchronicities in numbers show up in various different ways. But if you are seeing repetitive sequences like 111 or 555 they can hold meaning in love, relationships, or destiny. I am no numerologist, but I utilize the internet all the time when I am uncertain of a numbers meaning. Throughout the journey I found that certain numbers painted specific pictures for myself. So a number two for me means something entirely different for you. Our angels communicate with us in so many different ways, numbers are the easiest ones. Numbers hold power in our world. Remember these when you begin your journey or take on day to day tasks. Maybe you find yourself asking a question or making an important decision and see those numbers. Think of these numbers as a nice nudge. Pay attention, and reflect on your thoughts. Pursue it and maybe you will find the answers you are looking for. One night I sat on the floor to mediate and waited for my misty numbers to appear. Nothing. I squinted harder, and still nothing. I was a little disappointed, it was becoming so much fun to research the numbers that were appearing in front of me. But then it dawned on me that maybe it stopped because I had received all of the wisdom that was meant for me to see. It was time to listen and drive myself into action for the next task whatever that was to be. My quarantine routine was spent ignoring regular university and attending Tik-Tok University.

The abundance of quick information made everything so easy to absorb. With the help of the algorithm guiding me through rabbit holes I learned more in 10 minutes on that app than I did in 18 years of schooling. One rainy day a particular add popped up on my phone that sparked my traveling interests. It showed a farm in Hawai'i. It sparked a feeling in me that felt urgent. But I had no idea how I was going to do it. I started manifesting the island into my reality, even though it felt impossible to attain. Quarantine flipped the world upside down and my days spent in my parent's home were lovely. I felt like I was part of a family again, something that I had not felt in almost all of my remembered life. But I needed to get out, and I thought what other dream life to live than in Hawai'i? The next day I woke up to attend a zoom conference on sustainability in the NFL. The speakers for the conference had decided to put up one of the green screen backdrops with palm trees. As they began their talk, they introduced themselves by saying "hello everyone thank you for attending! We, uh put these palm trees up to give you a little bit of Hawai'i to relax you for our speech today." And I thought, how strange? What a coincidence, at the time I had thought. I move on to my other daily tasks, running, throwing clothes on the floor, eating all of the food in my fridge, and eventually sitting down to scroll through social media. The first three pictures posted were tagged with a location pinned in Oahu. For the second time that day when I normally never see or hear anything about Hawai'i, the island was brought to my attention. I set my phone on the table and head out to the mailbox to get the mail. I hadn't spoken to the neighbors much before, we were new to the neighborhood and we just so happened to be crossing paths at the same time. We start talking a bit about random things and she explains how she was engaged and that their wedding was pushed back. She was upset because she was unsure about whether or not she would be able to go on her honeymoon. And where was the honeymoon? Hawai'i... Three times in one day, the island called out to me. I felt her coming closer, as I sat down in front of the couch to put on something to watch on TV, a commercial for property in Hawai'i comes on. I turned off the television and ran upstairs to my computer. It was a sign clear as day. I was going to go, I had to whether or not they understood. That same evening I booked the flight and made the announcement to my family that I was leaving. They were not happy and were so controlling they almost decided that I would not be allowed to go. But I had to, every bone in my body was already there. My memories which hadn't happened yet. Every cell in my blood knew that was where I had to be.

VI

Finding the Self

HE ISLAND'S HEART called out to me. Her soul was calling my name. Hawai'i began popping up everywhere in my day to day life. Not simply because of the algorithm on my phone. She was everywhere and I could feel the excitement coming from her heart. So, for the remaining rest of the time I resided at home continuing with my quarantine routine I had started at my dumpy college apartment. I was never in the house bored. I was learning. I finally understood the phrase, "using technology as a tool." Tik-Tok university helped me learn and understand myself. It was on that platform that I learned everything about my shadow, my ego, the chakra systems, erased history, astrology, and plant medicine on a deeper level. It brought me to boundless information that I never would have had access to before. Spiritual Tik-tok brought me to different books and more information faster than ever before. My entire journal was filled with notes. Every day was a new mind-blowing fact. I was ready for whatever life was bringing me. I began to practice manifestation again. Began to do what everyone was saying to do on the app which was to follow my dreams. Specifically

49

dialing in on all of the details, what did I want? I craved real deep friendship. I dreamt of a perfectly balanced group of girls. People who were spiritually aligned with where I was. I dreamt of connection to the earth, adventures like I had seen only in TV. I dreamt of nights spent dancing and playing under the moon only ever stumbling into more fun. Hot romance in a true gentleman warm to the touch. Someone who opened doors and buys flowers. Someone who could sing, love with a kind heart. I was taking off with no thought that my feet would ever touch the ground. Who would have thought that all my dreams would come true? Two weeks were up, and I was back strapping into my home-made stitched mask. This time, not as jenky the one my dad made for me the first time around. The airports were a dead zone. I booked a connecting flight and was really hoping I would get a decent meal, but everything had ingredients that I could not eat. I was starving and tired of wearing a mask and to make things worse when I arrived in the airport for my transfer, I realized I messed up the connection. It wasn't a two-hour difference, it was 12. I was too cheap and broke to pay 200 dollars for a hotel room and Uber back to the airport in the morning, so I stayed up for another twenty-four hours alone in the LAX airport. When I say alone, it was me and the janitors hanging out around the terminals. Super apocalyptic. The lights flickered; the food vendors weren't even open. Atypical 24-hour zoo turned silent. I knew my parents would be wondering when I would be landing about halfway into my realization that I would be waiting in the airport for a whole day so I lied to my parents and told them the flight was bumped up because I was too embarrassed to admit my failure to them. Failure was what they were expecting, and I was not going to allow them that satisfaction, but I was also intolerant to my vulnerability. Lying was easier than admitting that

I had made a mistake. Lying was always a lot easier than failing for me. But by lying I was failing myself in more ways than a simple fib about my flight. A miserable 24 hours later I had finally gotten to fresh air. A warm welcome was felt in the itching, inflamed and irritated mosquito bite on my right forearm. And a smile from the girl standing next to me at the terminal exit. We were so drawn in smiley and bold enough to introduce ourselves to one another. We just so happened to be moving to the same exact part of the island living within five minutes of one another! Her aunty pulled up to pick her up from the airport. As we hugged goodbye, a young woman in torn rags carrying a cigarette pushing a shopping cart walked by. She stopped and began to shout out jumbled words, which was startling to me. But aunty was unfazed, "give her love." Give her love? I never heard anyone say that before. Give a shouting homeless woman love? I agreed, but I was shocked that aunty was not even phased. We all began to shout, "GIVE HER LOVE." The energy the island was bringing me was all love. Shouting to me her shining abundance. All love. Even as I began undergoing a mosquito attack. I had grown to form five bumps enlarging by the second by the time my new friend had left. Still waiting to get picked up, I pictured what my new home would look like. I was itching at more than my mosquito bites; the excitement was killing me.

Still not completely able to overlook the physical itchiness on my arms I began to ponder the silly comparison between these blood sucking bugs and my parents. Always hovering over me. Except my parents didn't give me irritated and itchy rashes from their bites. Instead their impressions were left on my DNA.

When getting a mosquito bite the best thing to fight off the itch is to ignore it. Which is sometimes easy because we can physically make ourselves mindful enough to forget that it's there. Enough to ignore the pain. Turning off the switch. Our brains have this ability, to turn on and off our switches with or without our direct attention. My ability to ignore mosquito bites was the same as me ignoring my traumas and pains of the past for half of my life. I desensitized myself to details in order to avoid whatever feelings may have come with those thoughts. What I mean by desensitizing was how much I had destroyed all the six senses that I had. I turned off way more parts of my brain than I realized. They say not to 'sweat the small stuff' but I wired my brain as a kid to ignore all my attention to detail or any of the 'small stuff'. They call it survival mode. It is a defense mechanism, that our subconscious brain does to protect itself. With mosquito bites I did anything to ignore the itching. With my problems I did almost anything to avoid them and push them out as so to forget the traumas and pain that was still a part of me. General education tells us about human evolution and the fight or flight response which is a physiological reaction that occurs in our brain in response to a perceived harmful threat to our survival. Our trauma takes away our childlike purity by conditioning us to live in fight or flight mode (fear). This trauma causes our amygdala to flip the switch, turning off our ability to explore learn and enjoy the world the way it was meant to be enjoyed. My trauma's accounted for a 15-year period of sleep. A period where I turned off my switch. That is until spirituality was brought to my attention. The idea of 'waking up'. Spirituality turns back on that switch and helps us to better understand ourselves. Understanding and breaking down our emotions. Why we react the way we react and how we can try to change those habitual thought patterns that have become our personality. Our personal reality. It is a state of being, a state of responses we have trained our self to believe as ourselves. When we are able to break free of this process and observe our reactions and the behaviors or emotions that come with it, we are breaking the habit of being our old self. By unlearning these patterns, we become more consciously aware of what surrounds us and begin to take things as they are, not as we think they might be. Spirituality helped me put the pieces of my life back together. I was sleeping for so long; I could barely remember my childhood. Diving into this part of the self I realized how much I was missing. I was still waiting for my ride to the farm, so I sat on the ground sifting through old home videos. The first one was a video of my dad dragging me and my sister around my childhood home on a blanket. Flinging us around as we screamed in joy. How did I not remember such a happy moment? I missed that utter fearlessness my inner child had. Someone who was gregariously loving and friendly to anyone. She was so daring and never thought to care what anyone thought, why waste time thinking about what others think? She was a restaurant owner, a mad archeologist, a musician, a dancer, an athlete, an innovator, an artist. She was animated, enthusiastic, overly trusting and friendly. She was a leader, a lover of everything. Her spirit was drug into the ground, and I cannot pinpoint exactly when. It was more of a gradual slump. I grew cold and cynical toward the world for a long time. I denied my inner child for so long but was finally able to hug her again. I was able to tell her I loved her; I forgave her. I cherished her, admired her and welcomed her back into my present. Waking up brought me to remember who I was before the trauma and how to grow to be the soul that my inner child always was. It is my truest belief that the children we come into this world as are exactly the kind of energy that the earth needs. Child energy. But not naive or immature. Pure, innocent, exploratory love. We need to remove ourselves from our fears, our shame, our guilt and our anger that replaced the innocence in our hearts. All the pain that made us grow cold and cynical. My inner child needed so much more than a big hug, she needed to be seen. To be understood and told that everything was always going to be okay. That she was supported when she built up shame for fear of being herself around judgmental friends. People who always seemed to leave her out. To be hugged in the moments she was forced into being the adult protecting her sister as her parents erupted in screams during their divorce. To be loved when she was sexually abused by a close friend. To be reminded that it was okay to be a kid, she didn't have to grow up so fast.

To be loved when she was confused about who she really was. To know that people weren't always going to take advantage of her. We all go through trauma. We ALL suffer and there is no such thing in comparison to suffering. Hawai'i was my medicine, my healing space to let the inner child inside me roam wild. She showed me how life is supposed to be. She showed me magic and fun. Free spirited and unconditional love. She brought me closer to spirit. Grew my soul. I was forgiven. The best thing we can do for ourselves is forgive and continue to love. Forgiveness is growth. By asking for forgiveness from ourselves and others we have harmed we heal and seal. Seal all opened wounds and heal the space between. If we can forgive our own hearts, for the mind and body's past mistakes brought on by our internal or external environment, then we begin the path to oneness. Full healing. Forgiveness to the self is like water. Water is formless. It does not take on the burden of being trapped to one mindset or one shape. Water adapts to the changes that it is thrown into. Water grows and changes, sure it has memory, but that memory is not dependent on its ability to grow into whatever it wants to be. My time centered in the middle of an island surrounded by water helped to shape myself into exactly the person I was always meant to be.

Settling in

The feelings of deja vu were creepily crawling all over my body. I was always meant to arrive on this island. The first two creatures I contacted on the farm were a grey and black striped tabby cat, and a white pawed, coated black one. They were nearly identical to my cats at home which truly freaked me out. As I scoped out my home for the summer it dawned on me that a 50-pound suitcase was not ideal for my 10x12 canopy tent. But I felt no shame. Propped up on a wooden platform was my bed and the remaining few feet was my home. The farm itself was tucked behind a yellow gate where the roads split off to give way to a luscious green valley covered in blue skies and cotton ball clouds. The clouds so close it felt like I was in the island version of a snow globe, where if you were to jump you might just reach up and touch the top of the sky. As the sun would rise behind the mountains it would strike the light reflecting a golden turmeric yellow. The lush mountain a bright valiant haze.

The roots of the trees would illuminate golden red, highlighting the dirt that sat beneath. The sun was hot, but it was the heat that I needed. It was snowing not too long before I left Pennsylvania, so the humid heat was more a breath of fresh air. I could smell the crisp oxygen radiating from the various types of trees. It was light and dense, not like the air in a forest. Soft sweet smells of fruits that I did not yet know were tickling my tastebud. It wasn't filled with toxic petrol or manure; it was real oxygen. A fresh and quiet getaway. Secluded and limited traffic in the valley allowed for a quiet I had never experienced. Hawai'i is the farthest landmass from any other landmass on earth and where I was in the valley felt just like that. Far away from all the noise. The noise from the pandemic which was becoming a new way of life. The noise of people who had no purpose being in my life anymore aside from bringing me down. The noise in my head with pressure I was putting on myself to figure out my future that seemed to have no aim. As I beamed around the 8 acres of land on the farm like a pin-ball machine, I only noticed the things that were familiar to me. Raised beds of crops and rows of kale, collards, beans, and lettuce. Herbs tucked away into the brown mulch. I realized I was racing through without noticing the details when I hit my face on the hanging purple bow that swings from the racks of ripening bananas on a tree. To be completely honest I did not look up at many of the trees at all. Not that I thought the orchard was for show, but I did not know what to look for. A lot of the trees and shrubbery at home are not fruit bearing. There was so much offered here. So many secrets to uncover in the land. All the details I was skipping over were the ones I was unfamiliar with and completely blind to. The wiring of my ADHD brain wistfully skipped over the details per usual. Noticing the detail of all the plants and animals was something I looked over and did not appreciate until I learned to love the land for all that it could share. I had always had a beaming appreciation for the earth, but I had no idea that she could be so plentiful. I could hardly believe such an astounding amount of abundance were in my presence. That I was experiencing the dreams I dreamt for myself. This feeling was as serene as my first sunset on the island. The most angelic art I had ever seen. I was experiencing color in whirlwinds of vibrant geometrical patterns. Some with fresh pastels that were highlighted by the glow of the sun. Cascades of rich greens, tender bronze. Honey clouds stretched their arms out to dance with one another over the peak of the mountain. As the sun grew lower shades of ruby painted over the original pastels. I was charmed. Head over heels for I was truly caught in the spell of the world. I finally felt my heart stretching far and wide for the first time. This was different than romantic love. What began ushering in was the divine understanding that every single thing is connected. I felt that entity. That interconnectedness on such a resonate level I could barely breathe. I was detecting all my senses at their maximum simultaneously. I could suddenly taste individual flavors of the food I had eaten earlier. The musky sweet smell of soursop trees. The sounds of the grass, trees, barely whistling for there was no wind. I was experiencing life to fractured abundant details. This high continued along my tour of the farm. Fields of red dirt where the clay was so fluffy, I never wanted to wear any shoes. The sun had dried up a lot of the grass staining them like hay where they rounded the edges of the clay path. Bamboo swayed in the east corner of the land where they would smack into one each other's sides. The bamboo grew in perfect segments. Not completely hallowed. The various sizes and thickness of the shoots would ram into each other to create a natural chime. I was awake and the world was with me. Inspired by this exultant new life I decided to stretch my arms in every direction. I wanted to write a song, I wanted to produce a sustainability video to showcase what I would be learning on the farm and prove to my parents that I was doing something useful with my photojournalism degree I wanted to learn to play an instrument, I wanted to explore create and love the island that ushered me to where I always dreamed of being. The first day planting was heaven in a hand basket. The universe brought me to precisely the perfect people to thrive around. I was greeted by a fellow east-coaster, someone so relatable it was almost terrifying. Up until that point I felt like a kid whose parents sat me in front of a bunch of candy and then told me to wait till they get back to eat it. I could not wait to bounce all my ideas out and talk about the spiritual awakening I was having, I had no one to relate to while I was home so up until that point I felt extremely alone. Time stood still for the entirety of the conversation. We both had recent break-ups, were on separate but similar spiritual journeys. Both equally as interested in each other. A real conversation balanced of listening and talking. The bond was instantly formed. We were going to have a grand summer. As I was introduced to all the others working on the farm, I found that all of us seemed to be in extremely similar circumstances. There were a handful of others but the most impactful were these three girls. We got along in the most balanced of ways. We were even elementally balanced astrologically (earth, fire, air and water.) The first night we all sat around the fire and smoked a little bit of ganja. As we sat in the darkness illuminated by the smokey glow. I was so gratefulness to be alive. I thought to myself... I really am smoking weed in the middle of the jungle in Hawai'i. I made it happen, I made it here. I was making my dreams a reality. The moon was so close. It illuminated everything at night. Her glow would make trees cast night shadows which really freaked me out at first. I was walking and kept turning around thinking that something was following me when it was only my shadow. Time stood still on farm time. Days on the farm felt like months. It was only one day, and we had discussed enough information about ourselves and the world for a lifetime. I had experienced what felt like multiple realities all in one experimental day. It was still only the first day. As I stared at my newfound soul friends against the embers glowing in the fire, I realized I was not really looking at them. I was seeing something else, a unique structure in their body. They looked like aliens. I blinked. I knew this feeling. I had seen this before, but thought I was tripping out too hard on the weed. With the spiritual understanding I had acquired I formed the idea that maybe I was not tripping out at all. I was staring at some form of an indigo ethereal body. It was almost like an exoskeleton but radiant with dusty light. It would happen a lot whenever I would deeply connect with whoever I was high around, like the level of comfort allowed people to drop their walls low enough for me to peer into their non- physical body. The euphoric feeling that draped over us was so strange. Since the pandemic I had not had so much social interaction, and it was liberating. To-be-in- agreement and understanding. The walls were down and all three of us seemed to somehow telepathically convey everything we needed to convey toward one another. These were the kinds of friendships that I had never experienced before. We questioned each other and were able to open-up about the vulnerabilities we had. We were supported and beyond open what anyone normal would be in the first ten hours meeting someone. The island brought me to these people with a purpose. Something like a soul family, but a little bit different. We all understood each other so well, we spoke each other's language of weird. If someone can speak your level of weird, it is bound to be for an epic friendship. We more than spoke each other's language we spoke understanding. I think there is a difference between simply speaking the same language and speaking the same understanding. Sometimes we can speak and not one person listens. But maybe they listen, and they do not understand. They perceive it with their own judgements and assumptions. They listen and try to make sense of what we say, then try to respond with the extent of knowledge that they have.

Well it seemed like for all of us girls we had a great, open minded understanding that paved the way toward instant connection. A synergetic meeting of people crossing paths at pivotal moments on our individual paths. The lifestyle that I dreamed up for myself was mostly becoming a reality. I was living out something big. I had no idea what I was even looking for, I just knew that whatever it was it was going to be great. At that time, I had so recently stepped into the realm of possibilities as far as freewill and power go on earth. I made a list of dreams up before I came and when all of them started to become a reality, I truly felt like I was wielding a magic wand. Living out this dream life was everything I had ever wanted.

Follow the numbers

In math class they teach us about numbers. They teach us names for them, and they teach us various ways that we can use them. But they leave out all the juicy stuff as if it were a secret. Numbers are meant to be more than a means to an end, a quota to meet, dollars to be had. Numerology is the study of numbers.

I first got into numerology because I was fascinated by the significance numbers had over people's lives. Where we live is comprised of a number when it is broken down into meridian lines. The day we are born are a collection of numbers. The information of the world is held up my numbers. Numerology and astrology are very similar but use different methods of approach to receive the goal: insight. There are things like the life path number, the expression number and heart's desire numbers. Numerology reveals numbers as trials and potential for every positive a negative. Numbers are messages from the universe. Numbers carry cosmic messages from our higher selves and the universe clueing us in on how we are doing. Mastering the numbers is lead through comprehending the meaning. In numerology 11 is a master number, it is said to hold a tremendously magnificent power. 11 stands for the illuminator, messenger, and teacher. Ever wonder why people make a wish at

11:11? It's a portal, that's where the "wives' tale" comes from. The number 11 is known for its connection to higher wisdom- psychic channeling from source. After about one week of my time spent, I had noticed I was seeing 11 everywhere. I would be focusing on something and would go to look at the clock at 4:11 5:11, 6:11 7:11 11:11. I felt so encouraged by the numbers, knowing that I was doing something right…Or something out of balance. I was freaked out, because it was happening ALL the time. I felt like I had mastered the art of time and that I was a wizard. The number 11 is one of many in whole with the universe. They say that synchronicities are messages worth tuning in to because they are messages from the divine asking us to pause and seek out what the message might be. Following the numbers mean, stop and think about what is being thought about and pursue whatever it is you might be questioning. I embraced this number as my guiding number and trusted that wherever I went if I just so happened be guided by 11 then I was following my purpose. As I came to realize 11 to be part of the arsenal along my journey, I thought to reflect in my journal to see what consistencies there were. I followed the date back to when I had first arrived. My flight was on the 11th of May, and my plane ticket? XVD11F. Numbers, do not lie. The immense strength and encouragement I would feel rushing through my veins with every 11 that passed by. It was not as if I were waiting around to see 11's. I would be working on a project or having a conversation and randomly without thought check the time to see an 11 glaring back at me. I knew big things were happening, but I was not entirely sure where or what that meant. I trusted that the universe was showing me the way with each eleven I felt as though I was turning my 11 sideways to climb up the tears on a ladder. With each eleven, a level up to my higher self and purpose on earth. The higher I climbed the stronger I became and more momentum I felt blowing me forward or upward. I usually set time to journal at the beginning and end of my day. But there was always something happening where I needed to write something down, so I took it everywhere. Fleeting thoughts no longer existed because they were floating through my pen and onto the page. Between breaks on the farm I often took to the moped to hit the beach. On this day I could not decide which beach felt right. I would stop, get out go to the sand and turn around and come back. By the time I reached the fourth spot I did not have much time to spend in the water, so I ran down to take a dip. I got out, sat in the soft blanket of land and rolled around like a dog. I was obsessed with the feeling of the sand against my body and I did not care that people were staring at me. I was enjoying the crap out of the beach, they wished they were that free. I had a little bit more time before heading back to work on the farm, so I brought out my journal to write. It was time to clarify some goals for the next few weeks. I knew I wanted to get better at surfing. I knew I wanted to radiate more positive energy and show more appreciation for the life that I was living so down it went. Pen in hand into the notebook. I glanced at the time, 4:11. It was time for me to go! So, I ran back to the moped reached for my key and nothing. The key was gone. In a full panic I threw everything out of my bag and into the busy street almost crushing my I-Phone. I took to the sand. In a frantic swirl I kicked around the spot where I was sitting. Nothing. Racing through my head, all I could think about was the money I did not have to pay for a replacement key. I stood up, "HEY!" Some families looked up, other random eyes on the beach turned my direction, "I lost my keys, can you please help me find them?" To my surprise, everyone started to help me look. We searched, dug around and up walks this man who had been gazing at me the entire time I was on the beach. He found, my keys. PHEW. I was so relieved, and almost late to get back to work. I was in a rush to leave but couldn't leave the prince hanging. He had thick curly dreads and was openly shaking with nerves. He was visiting from another one of the islands and was only in Oahu for the next few days.

He saw my journaling and wanted to find a reason to come talk to me, losing my keys gave him the perfect opportunity. He asks asks, "Wanna go surfing?" My jaw drops "I have a board for you if you want to go, I'll pay for a lesson." Five minutes before, I had written in my journal that I wanted to get better at surfing and in walks a man who wants to pay for a lesson??? Uh YES! I asked, and the universe answered. This whole awakening thing was great I got everything that I asked for, all that I manifested into real life. I felt the power within myself to accomplish anything that I desired. The numbers were in my pocket and I was guided by something much bigger than myself. I could sense it. It was more than a belief; I knew that things were all going forward in alignment.

Share with me the knowledge of the land

Let me feel the warm embrace from the sun wrapped around me
Like a soft blanket.
Blow on my neck and send shivers down my spine
Make me feel the radiance of livelihood
Allow me to breathe your pain
To relieve you from this uncertain future.
Let me feel the rain so it may bring me back to peace.
The shadow covers the night of the moon Illuminating the truth.
The crickets play in an orchestra all joining in unison
It continues, some join in later than others, some stronger, some faster
But in the end, they all create the same vibrational hum.
We should be more like the crickets all tuning in the same
Understanding the metaphors, secrets.
So many stories untold, unwritten, unloved.
How could anyone truly understand when she cries or when
she laughs when they do not know to listen.
We see, but do we understand? We think, but do we know?
Share with me the knowledge of the land so that I can share it
with you.

VII

It's not just about the self

VEGETABLES TO FEED the mouths of dozens of local families. Hawaiian soil nourishing people who bought from the small organic produce farm, the farm that I was working at. Free from chemical pesticides and conventional big-agriculture production. We supported restaurants, grocery markets, and the farmers' market. Cultivating land cultivates experience. In our separated western world, we are removed from this process. We fail to appreciate how much work it takes to produce enough food for people to eat. The farm was providing everything that I needed to grow and learn as a person in exchange for my time. I had rent covered and food on the table. Food that was grown out of a relationship with the land. All relationships in our lives are important. The relationship with our self being one of the most important, the relationship with those around us including friends/family of all kinds, and our relationship to the environment. The plants. The things that feed and nourish our bodies. Our being. Plants and humans were designed to be in love with one another. When the pandemic spread, I recall reading tweets about nature's quick come-back revival. Clean air in cities that had been smog covered for years, wild dolphins returning to the canals in Italy, the Himalaya's visible for the first time in a decade. The improvement allowed for the quick assumption that humans were the ultimate destroyers, and that "nature would be better off without us." Although while a reduction in carbon emissions and excessive human activity did allow for our earth mama to catch her breath, it does not prove that without us she would thrive. The earth and humans are symbiotic. Humans need plants for food, and plants need humans to keep them healthy and abundant. In a world where we will the plants to give us more, more and more without assessing what we need or how much is too much, we have disregarded the fact that all the plants wanted to do in the first place was give! You see, the more you pick from some plants the more they reproduce. The 'happier' the plant becomes! When the plants first start producing, they await a human touch. Green beans are a perfect example. During the first harvest we had gathered 10 total beans out of a little over 75 plants. The next day we returned to see the plants had given us triple what we had picked the day before. Plants can certainly produce and photosynthesize fine without humans. They can be watered by the rain and grow receiving the sun perfectly fine solo. But they care for us, they know when they are harvested with love energy. Our food system is so abusive today, the energy is not formed out of love. I always knew and respected the earth in the ways that I could, but farming brought in an entirely different perspective. We can bring our reusable cups and silverware all day long, but if we buy plastic wrapped processed foods or even order food out, we lose the vision and appreciation for the dish that is put in front of us. We see the result, not what it took to get there. Small farms are a rarity and I do believe that if we applied our resources correctly, we would be able to care for the land so much more. If only we took our time. Commercial farms encourage machine and production to meet 'more more more'. We are destroying what it means to be human. Technological advance has disconnected our way of being so disharmoniously. It has separated us as much as it has connected us. Technology in the way it is used today has removed us from physical contact with each other and the life that we interact with. Technology in the way that it is used today is not applied for our benefit. Technology, in the way it is used today, has removed us from life. This life we live is a quick, fast paced round trip where day after day we trap ourselves in a feedback loop. A life so distracted that we fail to recognize the beauty within ourselves or our surroundings. We have everything at our fingertips. Everything at the press of the command key. We expect nature to bow at the press of the button. Conventional stores separate us from the process. We hit command as we pick up each item on the shelf. A jar of peanut butter, a bag of bread, a box of arugula. We get everything we want on command without seeing the process.

We don't even know what goes into half the products that run the mainstream money flow. God only knows what horrifying science ingredients are hidden in those 'natural flavors'. Poison, and we are the science experiment. Organic food, real food, is a little bit harder to obtain and the labels are often clearer about where they get their products from. When we grow to connect to our bodies, our minds, and our spirits we realize the effects of everything we do. Including what we feed our body. If awareness is spirituality then it is my firm knowing belief that environmentalism and spiritualism are one in the same. As I farmed, I learned the difficulties as to why the prices are so high. I used to scoff at an organic 10-dollar box of arugula. But now, I understand why these things cost so much. Small farms being driven out by large monopoly corporations, who chemically spray, produce factory farmed cheap GMO toxic shit. Which is only the brunt of it. Small organic farms use less technology so something like that box of arugula I would pick up at the store, physically takes hours to harvest by hand to gather enough to sell. This peppery tasting rocket food is wild and abundant but not every leaf is even. It takes a while to harvest the right ones, making sure they fit the golden standard of produce today. The golden standard for food; perfection. But not all fruits and veggies are the same. Some get bitten or nibbled by bugs. Some a little sun burnt. For most of the leafy greens we would harvest on the farm all individual leaves were to be carefully inspected. Thoroughly pampered for perfection at the market or for restaurants. We would sometimes throw out what seemed to be perfectly edible. But we live in a world of perfection. A world that is so privileged to be able to decide that a perfectly healthy piece of kale with a bug's munch on the side, is not edible. Because we are so disconnected from the process we barely recognize this as a privilege. We keep continuing around the feedback loop where we go to the store and pick up our perfect vegetables. Working on the farm made me realize that the land is chaos. It's wild and difficult to manage to produce perfection for the market that exists today. No discolored carrots or bruised papayas. Nothing less than perfection. Technology and accessibility have taken us away from this process. The process of appreciating life that I do believe everyone needs. Maybe farm life is not for you, that's okay it's a lot of hard work. But I do believe that everyone can practice how much appreciation comes in the form of what they do. By creating intention around the processes, we do see around us.

We can practice anytime we get food from the grocery store or by going out to eat. As we sit down, we can order a soup and a sandwich. We can taste all the flavors and experience the nourishment that is flowing to our cells. We can question and ask if we know all that it took to get to our plate. We have the sandwich, which was brought to us by our server. The server waited in the kitchen, while busy doing other things for other people to bring out our sandwich. The chef prepared our sandwich to give to the waiter. The chef may or may not have known where the ingredients came from, but let's assume that he does. The fresh bread was baked by the baker, and the greens from the farm down the road. The tomatoes and onions were grown in a distant location but were brought by the weekly stock shipment. The vegetables took months to grow into wonderfully round, green, red, yellow juicy produce. They were not always plants, they started as little seeds planted in the dirt. That sandwich worked with so many hands before it fit into ours. Boxed and packaged shit takes that away from us. We see the result, which takes away the value of what it took to get there.

It's convenient and easy to go to the store, order on insta-cart, and consume whatever it is that we buy online. But if we find ourselves buying products we cannot grow at home, or make ourselves, always set aside time to read the ingredients. Learn where it came from. Setting the intention to thank the hands and love that gave us the gift in front of us. Intentionally giving what we have value. Humanity's attempt at computerizing the earth is failing at the same rate it is succeeding. The more people wake up and reconnect with the earth the closer we all are to connecting to source. The more people begin to focus inward and on themselves the less the material world matters. The more likely people WILL want to grow their own food. Waking up to conscious awareness is to saving the earth as peanut butter is to jelly. The bread the cosmic whole which binds the condiments as one. The earth is real as much as we are real. The earth is a living breathing entity not a machine. Not a tool to be broken into and thrown away after a good…what do I-phones do now? Last for a year? As a kid my sister and I would run around my backyard to catch lightning bugs and butterflies. As we grew older, they stopped coming around and I wondered why? Why would all the pretty butterflies not want to play in our yard anymore? As an 18-year-old female I learned that many butterflies were on the verge of extinction. But for me, I hadn't seen one around my yard in years I thought they were already gone. It was a result of climate change. But climate change is a big word that gets thrown around a lot. Climate change is the result of catastrophe over the stretch of a million different smaller events all collectively sharing the result of planetary destruction. All the smaller events snowballing into the next because we live in an entire ecosystem that is dependent on everything before and after to remain balanced. Butterflies were going extinct because of the use of human engineered chemicals, specifically Roundup (glyphosate) in agriculture. Milkweed is the caterpillar's favorite food and it grows like crazy near a lot of farmed fields. Industrial agriculture does not like anything else besides the harvestable crop. Anything that does not involve perfection. So rather than working with nature they genetically modified all the fruits and vegetables equipping them to handle the glyphosate. That way the process of spraying over fields only harms the 'weeds' growing throughout the land. Human engineered plants doused in chemicals survive, while the milkweed dies. No milkweed means no food supply for hungry and growing caterpillars. Terrifying chemicals is only the partial culprit driving these winged angels to extinction. Humanity's attempt at engineering a life that outsmarts nature will never be fully satisfied. Nature is imperfectly perfect because her chaos restores balance. Humans cannot outsmart nature no matter how many smart devices we create. Laziness and comfortability are two of the worst traits that we can grow to have. And that is exactly what the evil people in this world are banking on. I am not going to sit here and participate. I refuse to stay separated any longer. I kiss the earth and walk barefoot. I grow my food and eat the imperfections that come with it because I know nature is as it does. Who cares if the lettuce has a munch or two from a couple of hungry bugs. It's edible so long as you wash it, so why waste? Our survival depends on more people rising above the idea of "normal". Normality conditions us, traps us into reality. Or whatever normal reality is. When we challenge normal reality we rise above perfection. Above the idea that we can't eat lettuce with a bite taken out of it as if it didn't exist in nature in the first place. In the chaos itself!

VIII

Loving the Self

FOLLOW YOUR INTUITION. Let spirit fill you with gifts. Source love; the purist form of love. I was seeing the most beautiful land in the world every single day. She brought me for green misty mornings filled with chirping peacocks and hot humid air even before the sun would awake. Heavy wide-stretched sunsets that showed me the vastness of god's painting hand. For the plush and visible crunchiness of the veggies in the morning as the dew would roll right off dripping into the moist soil. That same soil that had managed to stain all my clothes no matter how many times I washed them. She breathed me in and brought me so much love. She healed me with the spirit of aloha. It was a beautiful exchange of energy. I was healing the earth by mending the land. Growing food to feed her people so she rewarded me with good karma everywhere I went. As soon as I stepped off the farm the magic of life became reality. With every single one of my manifestations revealing itself in my reality. Each passing day on the farm I would race to the rusty, mirrorless moped to get to my happy place. Deep in the soft crystallized sand where no one was around. Not a soul. I was one with the waves howling below my feet. The stillness of the breeze met my ears with such peace. In my time alone I would spend my time journaling all of my thoughts. Anything my thoughts would think was written in the best way I could find words to explain. It was about a month in and I realized one very specific desire was not being fulfilled. Sex. Yes. SEX. I was deprived of the very thing I was seeking out post break-up. And yes I was fine pleasing myself on my own. But I craved connection. Farm time and covid limited my social interactions in general for quite some time so I took it upon myself to download tinder. I had never swiped on anyone a day in my life but it seemed innocently fun to try. It was a thrilling ego stroke. I'd swipe right on someone who had already swiped right on me. I was being lured in by so many attractive faces and figures. It was liberating to feel beautiful, all because of a swipe. But I learned quick to never trust a dating app. You never know who is on the other side of a screen. The FIRST time I venture into the online dating world turned into my worst nightmare. I biked to the beach about 10 miles away that day and had no desire of biking back. A seemingly nice and super attractive young man and I had been chatting it up on the app the last few days. Around the time I got to the beach he sent me a text letting me know he was in the area, asked if we wanted to get together. I said sure, if he wouldn't mind picking up me and my bike. He had a truck, perfect! He would pick me up and take me home in my bike after we had our little date. I wait by my bike at the edge where the road met the sand. I gazed at my phone anxiously wondering when he would show up, this was my first real date. "Abbey?" I perk my head up and go to greet him in the car when my brow fuzzes. This was not the right car, there's no way. But how did he know my name? Everything was wrong. "Sorry, wrong car" I said. He smiles and says, "no, it's me David." Fuck. This was not the guy that I thought I was talking to. This one did not have light hair and golden island skin. No, this was a scrawny statured pale faced liar who was pretending to be someone completely different. At that point it was getting dark, and I had no intention of biking home alone at dusk. I felt so uncomfortable. I thought for a second, I would give this guy a chance after all I enjoyed our conversations over text. I was stunned, he was loading my bike into the back of his truck when I yelled, "stop!" Silence. I pulled my bike out of the truck and hastily peddled the ten miles back home in the dark feeling quite shameful for not investigating more into this guy before meeting up. My phone had died at this point so I could not call anyone for help back to the farm. Lesson learned, but not deterred. What a story, I grumbled to myself laughing at how naive I had been. Life is going to lead us to failure, but it does not mean that we stop. Why ask "why me?" when we can say thank God! We can take failures and use them as pushes. There is a familiar saying that my dad always used to say, Try! And if at first you don't succeed, try and try again. So, I did. I tried and tried a couple of times that did not really seem to work out, but I was searching for something…or someone. And after a few dozen terrible experiences that someone came along. At 8:11, I notice a match. Let's call him Josh. Josh lived on the other side of the island, so it was more challenging to get a time when we were both free to hangout for a few hours. On June 11th, it worked out. Instant connection sprung between us as he picked me up in his green cube of a car. I felt so free that night. There was hardly a break in conversation, it all carried through moment to moment so effortlessly. He brought me to the top of the mountain and showed me the best view of the city. He looked into my eyes and I could see his giving spirit, I had never met someone who had eyes as dark as him. Eyes so dark the color barely reflected more than what most people see. But I could see blue behind the darkness. Blue that he never believed me whenever I told him it was there. The more the night progressed the lighter I felt. So freeing and fun, I was so close to my true and highest being that night because I was not afraid. I felt a surge of freedom of expression. I was filled with love for myself but not only myself for him. I knew this soul in some other life. I was in full control of my power and sexuality. I felt his jaw drop and eyes pop as I threw my upper body out of the window of the car as we listened to some indie tune. We went on endless dates that night. Different lookouts to laugh about new stories. Different restaurants for more adventure. This connection unmistakably ended with the result I had been looking for. The moment we pressed against each other's lips was electric. A rush of power was encasing my spirit, my mana, (mana in Hawaiian means life- force.) when the lights went out. I knew my power was getting stronger, but what sort of a movie was this? Who was filming?

Nothing about this boy or this situation was real. It was all stuff I had dreamed up. But that was exactly it. This was only part of my potential as a sexual spirit. Mana is sexual energy because it is the life force energy we put into everything we do. I was putting in the work on the land and the land was giving graciously back to me. I was putting in the work on myself, so the universe gave me a gift. A dream I had always wanted, a caring and giving relationship like this one. Josh and I had a lot of fun when we would get together. Every date a new adventure. He was exactly all that I had asked for. It was excitingly scary. Again, why was I getting everything that I asked for? When I asked the universe for a man for the last three letters of the alphabet and he was it. He bought me flowers, treated me with the utmost respect, strummed beautiful music on his guitar. He was warm and kind. He surprised me with gifts and things that he knew I liked. He paid attention. The relationship was so thrilling, so fun but so short lived. I grew distant because it was too fast and so many other events outside of our relationship were picking up simultaneously. I got everything I had ever wanted. All the nights I would dance alone in my room thinking about dancing with my future partner to Frank Sinatra. The dates, the surprises. Every single time we spent together was special, flirty, fun. I was so freed, puppy love. But just as I settled into the happiness of the relationship, I quickly came to the realization that life is not supposed to be all that we want. The universe was bringing me those things to show me the paradigm I thought I wanted as my reality when I never needed any of those things at all, including my idea of a person. I'll have a huge place in my heart for Josh. I was swept off my feet. Literally, he always picked me up and took such good care of me. He came into my life and taught me lessons in the same way that I taught him. I think that in another life we agreed to meet on earth to help each other grow in our own ways. He helped me find my voice. To find confidence in my voice. On all our dates he would bring his beautiful wooden guitar. We would harmonize all night long as he strummed by the fire on the beach, on the edge of the most beautiful overlooks in the valley, and in his quaint bricked in apartment that was just as comfy as the vast world outside. Singing in front of others by myself was always hard for me. I did not have the confidence. Hell, I barely had the confidence to fully speak any of my truths. Why sing when you fear you are not good enough? Why speak when you are afraid of what people might think? As we sang, Josh would ease my nerves. My nerves made me forget most of all the words, but he was so talented that he would change the song and play a new melody making me feel less anxious for making a mistake. So comfortable around instruments and even more willing to help me find my voice. Vulnerability is strength and he helped me feel freer in those moments of anxiety. Those moments before you speak and almost stumble on your words. To get over that moment where the heart skips and sinks in a nervous unconditioned and unconfident manor. He helped me turn off the switch that cared about judgement. Because at the end of the day the only thing that mattered is what I thought of myself. How I thought of my voice and not about what others may have thought. He raised the bar and showed me the expectation that will need to be met in any relationship I enter. Women, men, and anywhere outside or between deserve a relationship with as much respect and fun as the one I had with Josh.

Opening new doors

As I mentioned, life was picking up fast. My time with Josh was coming to an end. The beautiful dynamic of friendship that was developed on the farm with the group of girls that brought me so much understanding in the world was also coming to an end. We shared so much together but were onto our separate ways. Another chapter was closing in the relationships I developed in my life and it was quiet on the farm after they left. It was never the same, the days were longer. They weren't filled with our jokes, pranks, or daily comedic commentary. The farm was a little too quiet. I was spending more time working on myself and my shadow, but nothing felt right. I did not feel like myself. I was almost stuck in my shadow; it wasn't just under review. That is until I started seeing beetles everywhere. They were landing on my arms all day. When I began taking notice, I brought out my pen to jot it down in my journal. A round green ladybug landed directly onto the page. That same evening, I reached out to a friend from home to immediately notice her necklace which was none other than a scarab beetle. This time there was no speculation, I knew right away. Another level up, another spirit guide. That fast? Intuitively I felt that these guides would come into my life as I was stepping through another door. Awakening my abilities and gifts. A warning to let me know that I was ready for new lessons. The beetle was there to remind me to remain steadfast in my goals. Everything was aligning so long as I kept myself in the love vibration. A great way to do just that. A yoga potluck party with great friends, food, and some bodily healing. A friend I had made on the island was hosting so of course I was going to join. At the potluck I found so many friendly open-hearted souls. It wasn't draining, it was fulfilling. Parties were so intimidating back home, and I do believe every female has felt this. That glaringly demonizing stare from a group of girls who judge you as you step through the door. Bad energy. But this was different.

Everyone made a dish for the potluck. There was so much love in socializing with people who enjoyed being themselves. Across the way I found that I was so drawn into a conversation with two older folk that reminded me of my parents in a strange parallel universe type of way. I opened to them telling them that my life felt stagnant. I am not quite sure what else to call this but fate. After only a short while of conversation they offered me a place to stay. A chance to work for them on their property.

"Sure, come pay a visit, our address is 11......" I almost choked on the air as they spoke those numbers out loud. 11? My guiding numbers. It was more than meant to be. Hidden hundreds of stairs up in the jungle was my future for where my life was taking me. A treehouse. I would be living in a treehouse. Up above one of the clearest beaches in the north shore I lived in a screened in cabin with the most extensive view of the ocean. The ocean's blue arctic ice turned deep dark cobalt the further you would gaze into the horizon. Tiffany in between. The clouds mirrored themselves not in shadows, but reflections of themselves. That is how glossy it appeared. In the trees, the sounds were magnified. I could hear speakers blaring from the houses below. The energy was alive. Dozens of species of birds cheering as if to welcome my arrival. The farther up the mountain the hotter it became, although it was even hotter below out from under the trees. The canopy between was cool and breezy. Greenery covered the place. It was a small food forest. Fruit trees were everywhere abundantly growing papaya, cacao, noni fruit, ulu breadfruit, mangos avocados, cherries. There were patches of growing greens in between. It was all hidden. If I had not worked on the farm before I would have never known to look at all the hidden secrets that lay around the property. Small patches of growing greens hidden between the trees. Bananas growing out ready to swing. Papaya's just in arm's reach. Here, they had a food forest. Permaculture design utilizes the natural order of an ecosystem by re-wilding the garden. There is no waste, it all regenerates like in the natural order of the eco system. We can harmoniously live in nature while growing our food on it too. We are so neat and organized in the way that we farm today. In rows, in beds, away from all the chaos. But nature is chaos and that is what permaculture seeks to implement into farming. A deeper connection with the chaos was exactly what I found here. It was in this new home, my tree house that I would find my truth. Another chapter was beginning, and I had all my spirit guides with me. Supported by my ancestors, the animals, my angels and the love of my growing mind.

Karma

After a long day of adventuring I took to the town to get some food with friends. Keep in mind that the North Shore is not a city that never sleeps, it goes to bed damn early. Especially during Covid. Everything was closed, and we were starving. Driving down the road we see the lights in the pizza place still on. We looked up their hours and saw that they were closed. But I thought they had to still be around. So, I mosey on up to the door, knock and ask for leftovers. Blank stares. Unabashedly I turned to walk away when I hear a, "wait!" I never turned around faster. FREE PIZZA. Ask and you shall receive I thought to myself. Kindhearted people still existed. An old version of myself might have never had the balls to ask in fear of them saying no. But this me, this expanded reality me, was going to ask and accept whatever answer came out of it. To thank them for the wonderful gift of pizza, I cheff'd up home-made chocolate to thank them for such a sweet deal. The next day I dropped it off on my way to pick up some things that I wanted from the grocery store. I walked in and meandered around to get some coconut water, fruit and other miscellaneous things. As I turned into the aisle, basket full, the man in line behind me asked, "What's your favorite candy?" "Reese's peanut butter cups no doubt." He left, came back to where I was in line for check out and put the Reese's up on the counter. He then insisted I put my groceries up onto the register. I was stunned that someone would offer to do something so kind with no expectations. A true random acts of kindness, not luck. I felt so loved. Kindness is the way of the world. Kindness is love in raw form because it is love in action. That man's selfless act made my whole day. It was all so strange how quickly the karmic circle flew back at me. I had gotten the pizza, given back to them, and I was then given again. Breaking down love is easy because it is the gift that keeps on giving. It is more contagious than any sickness I ever had. When we are filled with love, we have nothing to think but love. Love, no matter the source brings us high, seriously. It's a certain combination of chemicals released in the brain. Love is a pleasure high. Love is a soft and light brush over the skin. It burns hot and fills space. Love is not limited to romance; it is so much more expansive of a concept. Giving is all life is really about, as I began to cry with overwhelming gratitude for the simplicity of the act he waved, nodded his head, and spoke the simple phrase "Aloha." The spirit of Aloha brings the essence of sharing to life. Aloha 'Āina ('Āina is the word for land in Hawaiian). This phrase is foundational to the way that the Hawaiians live. It's about the community, taking care of one another. That is exactly how random acts of kindness reflect the spirit of Aloha. There is so much identity embedded in those words, healing, gathering, ritual, hunting, farming, singing, dancing. This phrase made me understand the importance of taking care of the land. It was always my fate to come here. I was called upon the island mālama 'āina (to care for, nurture the land.) To learn ways to sustain life. The only way we can sustain future generational life is by playing with the dirt. The soil is what nourishes the food we eat. By dancing in the water and protecting its sacred beauty. Water is the element that connects all life. By cleaning the dirty air that has been polluted by clouds of darkness. It is the duty of present people to guard the earth with the knowing that future generations will thrive. Enough with the greed. Enough with the hoarding. Planting a tree does not mean that we will always get to eat its fruit. Nature is so marvelous to us when we treat her with kindness. Have we learned nothing from Disney's Pocahontas? Every rock, tree and creature have a life, a spirit, and a name. Learning the names take time and walking the footsteps of strange lands helps us learn things we never knew we never knew. A western upbringing is one of many things but most significantly it's fast. I was rushing through life for so long without stopping to look. I did not know to look up before getting smacked by a rack of bananas, I was learning things I never knew I never knew. To stop and smell the roses.

In the Aloha spirit some friends and I decided to visit the historic and sacred valley by working in the botanical gardens as volunteers. The valley is recognized for its spiritual and historical significance, it was a Valley of the Priests. This land protects endangered species, and very rare Hawaiian plants. All the wonderful trees and spaces are labeled as to provide guests with the opportunity to learn their names. As volunteers we were asked first, before stepping into the space, if we would ask to be welcomed. A custom I learned coming to Hawai'i is one of asking for permission. By asking the earth for permission, we grant sentience into the exchange. Beyond what we see, is energy frequency and vibration. The energy carries itself through the life force frequencies that exist in our experience. Asking before entering any space is a good way to practice feeling that life force energy. Before stepping into the ocean make time to appreciate the space the water holds for us. The land is as evenly conscious as us. Simply because we can't see something does not mean it is not there. It can be hard to pick up on other frequencies or energies when we are still inconsiderate of our own. When we rush, we skip over how much we can feel. It is impossible unless we slow down to learn the skills associated with tuning in. Before entering the sacred gardens, we sang a Hawaiian chant. E ALA Ē. We closed our eyes.

E Ala Ē

Ka La I kahikina (ka-la-ee-kaa-hee-kee-na)

I ka Moana (ee-ka-mo-ah-na)

Ka Moana hohonu (ka-mo-ah-na ho-ho-noo)

Pi'i ka lewa (pee-ee-ka-lay-vah)

Ka lewa nu'u (kah-lay-vah-noo-oo)

I kahikina (ee-kaa-hee-kee-nah)

Aia ka la (aye-ah ka-la)

E ala Ē! (AY- ALA-AY)

A dear friend, Noelani Love, has a version of this song that I think magnifies the mana (power) of this song (in case you are interested in the experience!). Oli (chant) means awaken, arise. The sun in the east from the ocean, the ocean deep. Climbing to the heaven, the heaven highest. In the East there is the sun, awaken. Chanting, or singing has always been an important part of culture since the dawn of time. The mo'olelo is an expression. Storytelling. Language was shared through stories told in the chants. Oli sow rich history into thick deep shades of fabric. The mana of the Oli lies in the metaphors because they had not written language. So that chant, as simple as it may sound represented the grand moment the sun arises each day. Imagine appreciating such an event. Something we take for granted because it happens every single day. Their culture praises every element of life because everything has a spirit. The vivid details that arise from the lyrics in the Oli romanticize the beauty in nature. Every action of the whole earth is sacred. The sun rises from the deep ocean to the highest heaven. Awakening the earth with everything she touches. The crack of silence before the sun rises in the morning is the only comfortable silence. The first inhale before she peers up over the East to exhale breathing warmth into the birds who begin to sing their song. She brushes over the cool, damp earth giving it a nice hug. The roosters begin to crow. A mango might fall from the tree making a loud smack crushing the leaves beneath. The pasty glow that ever so gently caresses the trees highlighting its leaves' veiny skeleton. Golden streaks jut out and spread the warmth even further poking the bugs who start buzzing themselves awake. The sun rises in the east and climbs to the heaven to awaken the start of life. We chanted our E Ala Ē, our quest for permission into the space. When we began the air was completely still. When we sang, the breeze began to swirl around us, the sun began hitting my face and I felt the whispers of the spirits around me. I had chills all up and down my spine and again I started to cry. As we finished the birds began to screech. We were given permission. The valley said yes. We set the intention of asking for permission. Before taking something that is not ours, or going somewhere that does not belong to us, we ask for permission. Before entering a friend's house or taking a bite of their sandwich it is only just and fair that we ask before taking or stomping. Asking for permission in nature is something that we rarely think to incorporate because we have not been raised to respect nature. We have not been shown the ways of asking, we have been shown the ways of taking.

And so, we were welcome there. The spirits answered back. We spent the day clearing invasive species of plants who were taking over protected endangered species. So many of the plants in the islands of Hawai'i were brought there for foreign travelers who stole their land. They did not ask before bringing and taking things that were sacred to them. They did not ask before replacing and destroying. Places like the botanical garden center help to educate people about the faults of our ancestors past and what we can do now in the present to restore the beauty that these native plants have to offer. For working so hard the universe prompted someone to give me yet another a gift. The woman we were volunteering with decided to share Hawaiian ginger with me. A large pink pinecone and when squeezed oozes out this clear liquid that smells like honey and heaven. Not only did I receive the ginger, plant itself, but was given a new stalk to sow into the ground to reap more in the future. The promise of the plants. The reciprocal process that humans and plants must help one another. I was so grateful and excited to be given such a grand gift to take care of. The gift of life itself. But I made a mistake. We went home and I sat in the bed in the back of the truck. As we arrived back to the farm, I rushed out to the ground pacing to get to the bathroom and in the rush, I forgot to grab the ginger. I forgot about the gift. Unfocused and forgetful I did not remember to get it out of the truck. As I awoke the following morning, I looked all around my tent. The ginger was nowhere to be found and neither was the truck. They took it to the dump that day and gone went my ginger. It was my fault for being so careless. For being so inattentive. So irresponsible with new life. All summer long it barely rained on the dry side of the North Shore. It rained a total of two times during my farming days. The first was a luxurious downpour spent playing in the mud, but this time: the second, was spent walking the rusted moped a mile to the nearest gas station. Couple no cell-phone service to let anyone know that I broke down with a torrential downpour and you have yourself a day. After this I stopped seeing the number 11 and the world went dark. I fell into what seemed like a soup of lower vibrational lulls. I physically felt my body weaken, the fantastical luck that seemed to grace over me dissipated into anger and uncomfortably. Long days and nights of lonely torture. I was careless with the gift, so karma was kicking me in the ass. Truly, strange things started happening. I even sliced my fingers three times in one day as I cooked dinner, deep cuts too. I knew I was being dragged down but could not pull myself out. The wavering confusion swept over me. What was I doing? I felt as though I was floating around like a speck of dust. Getting kicked around, blown over to the next and the next. As much self-work as I was trying to accomplish, I was getting nowhere. It seemed I was making mistakes and upsetting people left and right. My bubbly light energy turned to dark stillness. Karma for the ginger. Karma for being so carless and I understood it to be that way. I knew it was my fault and I had to ride out the cycle of my actions until it was balanced again. Until I had paid enough in unfortunate circumstances to make up for my blunder. The ego self is the part of us which guises itself, as the self. A separate part of the whole consciousness. Our individual identity. The ego in its guise casts a shadow. Shadows are something that creep out from behind us. They follow us wherever we tread in the light. Forgetfulness was a big part of my shadow. When we enlighten ourselves, we cast away parts of the shadow that no longer serve our purpose. At this point I was so ready to let go of being forgetful, to consciously direct my effort into becoming someone who remembered. Someone who stuck by their words and promises and stopped forgetting.

When we speak things out into the world and happen to not fulfill them, we barrier ourselves worthy of the universe's gifts. How will anyone including spirit know to trust our decisions if we keep on forgetting to fulfill what we spell out into the world? So, I began to change the way I approached forgetfulness. Rather than getting mad, frustrated, or upset at myself for forgetting. I decided to thank myself for remembering no matter how big or how small I approached it with love. The mistake I made with the ginger was karma's way of kicking my ass into gear. If I kept continuing with my forgetful ways I would continue to fall into deep lulls of soupy nothingness. I would stay in a lower vibrational realm that felt like a dark abyss. Working through the ego usually brings about strange dreams, and I knew I was getting somewhere when I fell into the dreamscape one night and was in something dark. Warm and filling. My ears were picking up the sound of thumping so loud I thought it was a train going by. But it was not quite so harsh, it was gentle although the volume was strangely extreme. It was not a train; it was my mother's heartbeat. It was me, inside her womb. The first moments of life as a little bean in my mom's stomach. The minute I identified with the situation I was brought to another sound of a heartbeat. But this one was my own. Slow breathe was being carved out but I was not gasping for air. It was still dark, but I heard the slow blip from a heart monitor taking its time, steady. It sped up, and up and up until everything became bright white before, I awoke to complete darkness. I felt my arm. I felt my chest where I had left my rose quartz crystal to sleep with. I was alive. But I had felt my first and last moments in life. It was working, the shadow work. My ego was trying so hard to keep the identity I had developed around myself. The identity that I thought was me before waking up. I was being reborn. I was ridding myself of the inhibiting thought patterns and beliefs I no longer needed or wanted in my life. The disempowering shadows which kept me from reaching the light and my purpose on this earth. Ego is fear. Ego is forgetfulness. Ego is hate. Ego is judgement. Ego is jealousy. All of the shadows lurking underneath our feet bringing our hearts down and out from the light. When we work through this, we learn the value in the self but recognize that our individualism is part of the collective whole. Priding facing our problems and talking through them rather than not knowing or ignoring the work that needs to be done. Letting go of the idea of ourselves, the story we create to hide from who we truly are. The real "I AM". Some of the most powerful words in any spoken language. We tell ourselves that "we are" this way because of that. That way because of this. It is time to work through the shadow and stop the habits we created for ourselves that keep us from the light. The stories that hate, judge, or fear. We must let go of who we are to become the person we are meant to be.

IX

Letting go of the self fear, hatred, judgement

THE FIRST TIME I felt independence from my parents was felt in two small etched lines near the soft center of my right collar bone. A cross tattoo. Freedom I wanted and freedom I felt as I had just turned 18 and knew my parents' resentment with tattoos, "It's permanent and it's disgusting," they would say. Raised Christian, in my mind at the time I had thought out the plan that if I got the tattoo and they just so happened to find out that I got it, they couldn't really get mad at me because it was a cross! It just makes me laugh, that I reached my hand out far enough away from my parents but with enough of a safety net boundary of approval. How daring of me. The over-bearing love they had for me only ever wanting to protect me from all the painful things that existed in the world. It was choking me. That controlling feeling was what pushed me from confiding in them.

I had this fear that they would not appreciate me for who I was.

This fear that kept me from being vulnerable or sharing anything with them. I hid almost anything from them because I did not want them to judge me. I knew they loved me but I did not want them to know that I made mistakes. Or that I made any poor decisions because that is exactly what they expected from me. Failure. I was almost paralyzed by the fear of failure because all I wanted was to succeed. To be perfect. I was fearful of other's interpretations of me not only my parents. I was a liar because I did not like owning up to my mistakes. I lied about almost anything to keep my reputation intact. I lied to myself, my closest friends and family. I was lying to everyone because I did not feel as though my true self was good enough. Lying demonstrates weakness because it reflects our inability to be courageous in owning up to our decisions. I lied to ease my own guilt and avoid punishment. My fabrications were ruining my life. In my attempt at being perfect I lied to everyone I knew and self-sabotaged my own life by pushing everyone away. But that fear of perfectionism is what drove me to change. Because when we change the way we look at things the things we look at start to change. My fear of failing slowly dissipated, because the more I lived the more I saw. The more I saw the less I cared and more I believed in myself. The past failures which were a part of my life were lessons and nothing more. We can make mistakes, but it does not mean that we fail. Rather than viewing life in successes and failures I began seeing them as humbling experiences. Humility is accepting that we do not know everything. We can be humbled in our mistakes and we can feel humble about putting love out into the world. Humility is surrendering to all our imperfections in whatever form they exist. Every decision that we decide to pursue can be a humbling learning experience FOR us. We have no reason to truly fear anything that happens to us when we seek out the light. When we understand that we as humans were never going to be perfect. That all of our decisions are the right ones to make and unfold on our beautiful path. This brings me peace. Knowing that as we relinquish all fear and trust that the universe always guides us to what is best for us. Even in times of trial, this brings me peace. When we drop the facade that fear holds for us our hearts can grow twice the size. Doubt tricks us into falling back into a state of fear but we can learn to outgrow that feeling. I stopped doubting and started believing because I had nothing to lose. I found myself and my truth. I disciplined myself knowing that so long as I kept my intentions pure that I had no reason to fear anything coming my way. We can outgrow doubt and step into knowing.

Knowing that we are protected and divinely guided. A Knowing that there is no such thing as mistakes, only lessons. A Knowing that there is no reason to fear even the most feared ticket out in life, which is certain. We are eternal beings. Death of the soul does not exist. There is no reason to fear when we are aligned with God and spirit. Death is an experience in the same way that all the emotions we feel are in and of themselves individual experiences. The everlasting essence of life flows within every soul. Judgement day is every day, not only when we die. Judgement is every day because anytime we make a decision the implications fall on us whether that is in this lifetime or the next. Every time we make a decision exercising our own free will we are essentially deciding our own fate. If we choose to steal, lie, or behave in a non-loving vibration then we demote ourselves from enlightenment. We whether our own souls with poor alignment of choices. Judgement is separate from the way we judge. Beliefs are an interpretation of life. This book is my take on interpreting that life. I do not have any better or worse idea than anyone else interpreting their lives. Judgment is the process of dictating how another person might think about their own life. We are all on certain points in our path for a reason, we are all students of life. When we judge people, it is because we believe their belief is not the truth. We are no more or less than anyone, any single being on this earth. We all are spirits growing and learning in every moment. Creation is perfect and made this earth imperfect because creation already knows perfection. When we judge others, we remove ourselves from love. Judging is different than knowing. When we meet someone, we watch them, listen to them, and come up with an idea of who they are. Compartmentalize their persona into a box that makes sense to us. We can make those assessments based off of things we already know. Evaluation is not the same thing as judgement. The knowing guides us closer to the truth because we feel out a person or situation for exactly what it is, and where they are at in their journey. People judge when they misunderstand. People judge when they judge themselves. Judgement is a roadblock on our way to self-love. If we are endearingly critical of the ways that others look, it is often because we are harsh with how we look our self. When we judge ourselves for the way that we look we are looking at a reflection of our own self-hatred. Judgement is a negative thought pattern that must be let go of in order for anyone of us to move forward in elevating our consciousness. For a really long time I hated the way the world worked. That was because I could not change it. I could not alter the fact that people I walked by passing in the street were unawakened. That the people walking by were stuck. Because they did not even know they were stuck. I hated that the world could be as filled with the love that I was feeling. I hated that it did not fit my vision of perfect. But that is when I realized that life is not supposed to unfold within our vision. This is the creator's divine plan. We exercise our livelihood as we do, and are all learning different lessons. We all experience the journey differently. Hate is nurtured and festers in the soul with intention. Hate is an emotion that seems fair. It seems fair because we see how hateful others can be. We see things and deem worthy of hatred because it does not fit our vision. But it is not about what we see other's experiencing. It is about the way we experience them experiencing. If we judge or hate the world for the way that it is, it is sure to hate us back. If we judge people for where they are at then the universe is sure to judge you for where you are at. This life is not a competition. We cannot fight the judgement of the world with more criticism. The more we judge and hate the world for all of the hate that exists the higher the flames will surge. We are stepping into the knowing. A time without fear. A knowing that we have no reason to fear, judge or hate any other individual experience. This is the age of love. The age of truth. Healing is a process which is not linear and the only way through is love.

Embracing Change

Take a second and look at your own eyes in the mirror. Don't look at the scar on your chin, the acne on your nose and forehead, or the hair that caresses your face. Gaze at the reflection in your eyes and really ask yourself, "who are you?" Do you even know how powerful you really are? I'll give you a tiny example. Have you ever been doing something in the store, maybe get the feeling you are being stared at only to turn and look directly into the eyes of someone else staring right at you?

This is something known as gaze perception, our brain cells have a precisely sensitive response to the gaze of others. Everyone does this, whether or not they are conscious of it. That evolutionary ability we have to sense something as distant as a gaze is a small peak into the powers that reside within us. If we can sense this energy without even having to think about it imagine what is possible for the things we do think about and notice. It is no coincidence that the minute we turn our heads we meet another pair of eyes facing our direction. Whether or not the other person realizes this, as they gaze toward us they are projecting thoughts. Those thoughts may be intentional or they may be unintentional. Sometimes the energies are positive and sometimes negative. Setting intentions in everything we do makes life all the more magical and appreciative. Intentions have the ability to destroy as they do heal. Anyone can have sprezzatura but, even effortlessness takes intention. We send our energy with our thoughts to everything that surrounds us. When we take the time to purposefully send that energy with intention we come to understand how powerful our thoughts are. Our alchemy. This is a habit that transformed my life. It might seem so silly at first but being grateful in every moment lifts our vibrations up. We see the world in an entirely different way when we create intentions around our crafts. When I make my breakfast in the morning I put love into it. I think nourishing thoughts. I imagine the food tasting sweet, filling. I imagine the food breaking down sending energy to the rest of my cells for the day ahead. I thank all the hands that went into growing and getting the food to where it is on my plate. Then I eat it. I put the intention into the food knowing that it was going to be great and it was. This is not the same thing as putting up expectations. I was not expecting anything from the dish. I intentionally poured love into the dish because I wanted to receive that love as I ate it. We can do this with everything. When we wake up with intention everything that surrounds us becomes a magical ritual. Each moment is the only moment we are ever guaranteed, by putting out appreciation for what we are given we transform ourselves. Stopping for a moment, in each situation we are in and reminding ourselves of what we are actually doing. "I sit in a comfortable hammock swinging in the trees reading a book beneath a mountainside. My belly is full. I am breathing. I can blink my eyes." Having the ability to feel all of the senses in each moment and putting the intention out there that we are ALIVE.

We can send love to the water we drink and the way we brush our hair. We can send love to the canvas we paint in life and the colors come alive. We can form intentions, but we can also absorb them. Like I said, we are powerful beings! If we can dish it out unknowingly we can take it in the same. What sorts of intentions are we receiving them? We receive messages from anything we interact with. Music being one of the biggest control systems. Music makes us feel things, and it is not simply because the lyrics are sad or the tune is slower. The frequencies of sound in the music can really hurt us. The words can hurt us because our subconscious is always listening and picking up subliminal messages. If we are listening to music with angry intention then we may in turn project a lot of anger out into the world. Our body internalizes everything we interact with. We have to be careful with what intention we put out just as much as what we take in. If we are taking in life that has hateful energy we will be a reflection of that. We have participated in habits for an unhealthy amount of time that are destroying our connection with the light. Breaking that cycle and getting uncomfortable with the way the world works, and the way we feel about things is the only way we will ever ascend to a higher level of consciousness on a personal and global level. We free ourselves from suffering when we let go of fear, hatred, jealousy and judgment. When we break our comfortable ways of living. History repeats itself until we learn the lessons we are supposed to learn the first time around. First the universe whispers. If we ignore the whispers then she screams. If we still ignore the screams expect a nice whack from a 2x4. Breaking habits and changing ourselves is painful. Avoiding the whispers, screams, bumps and bruises is somehow easier for some people than facing what it is they have to face. They say that life is suffering- but I truly believe that it is our responsibility to free ourselves from it. We free ourselves by working out our shadow and stepping into the light. By heeding to the whispers of light that sustain our very existence. Ignorance is not bliss. Bliss is the state beyond ignorance, it's waking up. Ignorance is comfortability in knowing the truth and not doing anything about it. I started doing something about it when I stepped into what made me feel uncomfortable. At this new refuge, I found a home in what I was resisting. I found a new groove. I felt light as a feather flowing along perfectly with the universe. I had time to play in the ocean surfing and splashing around. I was learning about the land in a different way, taking care of the space that provided me a home in exchange for my rent. Sunshine state of mind I was living in the present moment. Learning and changing more and more every day. Challenging myself every single day. Every time we step out of our comfort zones we are expanding our consciousness and screwing with the matrix. Conquering our fears, facing the resistance of unknown. One day I was biking home from work and decided to stop in the grocery store. I bought a jar of peanut butter and some grapes. As I was leaving there was a busted up gold truck with a pleasant looking man inside. For some odd reason I had the feeling that I needed to talk to him, and that there might have been a reason for it but decided to go against it and pedal on. When I thought to myself no and ignored it there was a huge line of traffic that suddenly appeared on the non-busy street. One car passes, then another one and another one. Then I get the idea that maybe this is a sign to go back, stop, you must talk to him. Well, as I turn around I realize he is going in the store and I get second thoughts. Are you crazy? Why are you talking to this person? Even though a voice came into my head that was not my own and urged me to speak to him. "Seriously, what willed you to try and do this." I thought. I had absolutely no romantic intent, he was attractive sure but not the kind of person that I would pursue. He went into the store, and I decided to wait by his truck. At this point, I was just being ridiculous. I hoped that I was right by listening. He approaches his truck. "Uh hi, this is going to sound wackadoodle," Oh great. I think to myself. Why in the world did I say that...When have I ever used that word before? "I had this feeling that I was supposed to talk to you." He stares, as his face turns pale he places his groceries into the bed of his truck. Nothing but awkwardness fills the air because I had no idea what I was going to say. I mustered up the strength to reach out my hand and attempt at asking him random questions that went nowhere inspiring. It went really nowhere at all. It. got real awkward when he took to the short-lived conversation to be a romantic gesture and shyed away saying that he had a girlfriend. He left and I sat in the Foodland parking lot cracking up that I had no idea what had just happened. There was no reason at all, it was a joke. A funny that the universe was playing on me because they wanted to make sure I was listening. Maybe in that dense moment where blank smiles and stares fill the air with awkward breath, I found myself a home. A home in being uncomfortable. Of talking to anyone and everyone outside of our circles. Being daring enough to be friendly and kind to every soul that we interact with. Every day became a game. I would set out to reinvent myself by connecting and sharing my light with as many people as possible. What new questions could I ask people? How many different types of conversation could I have? I wanted to explore the world of questions. I am so sick and tired of "How are you?" When was the last time anyone answered that question with a "I am doing so bad, you?" I find that making a statement or exploring a different set of questions is more engaging anyways. I like to ask what people had for breakfast. Then ask them more about it. I like to ask what people are working on that makes them happy. I began expanding and growing with more and more people even if it made for the most awkward conversation in the world. Aside from how are you, there are tons of conversational language that does absolutely nothing for humanity. One being the passion question. "What are you passionate about?" Well if you are anything like me, you are passionate about a whole lot of things. Passion is a 'strong and barely controllable emotion'. So, why are all of us following something that we can barely control! We are following the pursuit of suffering by allowing our 'passions' to dictate our lives. When I got to college all anyone wanted to talk about was career goals, "What do you want to do with your life?" or, "What career do you see yourself in with that degree?" For me it was never about the objective. I had my mission that I had stuck by ever since I can remember. "Travel the world and help people." Is how I would respond. Though I had no logistical way of doing that with a degree in photography. I wanted to really help people and somehow, I knew that I was going to make that happen because it was a mission, not a career. I see people get so lost and wrapped up in having to decide based off of their passions and education. They get lost in the idea of a career. Whenever anyone would ask me the passion question I would simply respond with a smile and a, "just going with it." Life brought me that far happy so I couldn't think of a better way not to stress about how I was going to achieve success in life. Instead of asking children, teenagers, high schoolers, even college students what they wanted to be when they grow up, we should be asking them if there was one problem in the world that they could solve what would it be? If we could stop asking what people are passionate about and instead asked them about their life story. If instead, we asked them what brings them love because I bet, they have tons of passions! Music, dancing, art, film, video games, math, cooking, surfing, language, hiking, building, gardening! The amount of passions any one person can have, is endless. Being passionate about something you love is different than following your passion of love. A passion is not the bullseye on the target, love is. Now we know that emotions are energy in motion. If passion is an uncontrollable emotion, then all our passion is energy turned motionless. If we stop asking the passion question maybe, we can learn how to be passionate about what we love. What we came here on earth to do. If we all spent a lot more time being passionate about what we love and desire, then we would be living in harmony. We are all a piece to the puzzle with our separate purposes and skillsets. We all need each other. I truly believe if we were all passionately pursuing what we love then we would all benefit perfectly from the skills that we all share. We would have everything we need. So much of the lifestyle I lived was based off bartering and trade. Everyone had a skill and utilized that skill to benefit one another. Everyone with land trading what they grow. Some of my friends were chefs who would bake nice breads and create the most decadent cakes in exchange for yoga classes. Some of my friends would trade jewelry in exchange for fresh fruit. I was trading my time for rent on the island while pursuing what I loved which ended up being writing this book. When we perfect skillsets or crafts they become desirable and exchangeable. As my life continued to thrive I nestled into my purpose. I did it by asking the right questions. Asking for clear signs and learning how to ask the right questions can be difficult. Being inquisitive and being specific with what we ask invites more specific answers. I used to ask questions like "should I do this" but the more I grew in communication with spirit the more I realized my "should I" questions were never answered. There is no should. We have free will and should implies rightness. We could do anything we want, there is no right answer. Recall the fork in the road. One of the paths might get us there faster, and the other makes for bumps and bruises. But we get to the end so long as we choose one, there is no right path. The more specific we get, the clearer the answer will be...Most of the time. Because at the end of the day the answers are always within us. There are many ways of going about seeking the answers to the questions. Some of us may shuffle music and find that the answers we seek are messages in the music trying to tell us something about our question. Some of us may use tarot decks to ask questions, and in my experience the tarot deck never lies. Some of us can light candles and feel the physical presence of spirits around us. We may ask 'yes' or 'no's' by requesting the light be flickered for yes and still for no. Some of us might just ask the universe and find that the answer reveals itself in a few days. Patience is key, not all answers are meant to be known right away. We do not get to know everything right away, because we have to learn to heal ourselves first. I found that I had many blockages along the way, karma from the decisions I had made in the past and other blockages that exist in the world we live in today. Blockages that formulate in the body from the way we eat, sleep, and exercise. Blockages stemming from unhealthy habits of lying, cheating, and stealing in the past. Stealing shows the universe that we are not yet ready to accept what she gives to us. Lying creates a synthetic image of ourselves and what we do which is not one of god's image. Lying cuts us off from our most authentic self. Cheating is unfair because it is a manipulative way of getting what our lower self (the ego) wants. That is not part of the love vibration. Understanding that these are all habits that we have to be willing to break. All parts of the ego that weigh us down from leveling up. It can be so hard to learn how to both let go of what no longer serves us while also learning how to wield the power that follows a new level up in the spiritual adventure in life. Always new lessons to be learned, sort of like in a video game. Beginners getting beginner lessons. Advanced players fighting harder battles. It never stops. It's always a test. Leveling up and choosing to heed to the call following the whispers wherever they lead us. Who wants to get whacked by a 2x4 every so often? Listen to the call. Master the art of distraction. Distraction is easy. It is so easy to sit down to do an assignment for five minutes and pick up the phone to scroll on social media for a half hour. It's easy to distract ourselves from anything that we want to do. It's easy to spend time avoiding things, procrastinating. Time is so valuable, and it is on our side so long as we put one hundred and ten percent into everything that we do. The way that my brain is wired allotted me a different set of abilities when handling distractions. Rather than trying to do things like everyone else thinking for a minute that I was broken, I used distraction to my advantage. I called it my flow. When I would sit down to do a task like writing this book, I would have several things around me all at once. I would have my phone but not for social media but for music if I wanted to turn something soothing on in the background to ease the stress of outside noise. I would have my journal next to me in case I started to feel shifted and out of focus I would mark it down in my journal. If I felt the need to exit 'the zone' then I would pick up my pen and write down all the words describing how I was feeling. Then I would break that down. Scattered. What about my life feels scattered? Sometimes I would feel scattered because I was taking on so many projects and could not get them all done in a reasonable manor. I found a true home. My first and only place that I ever felt like I belonged. I was never dry of plans. I made friendships all over the island and fell into the trap of distractions once again. I was enjoying myself a little bit too much. Spending nights at heavenly retreats, jam and smoke sessions that lasted till the morning, swimming with all the sea creatures, moon festival activities, adventures all around the 'aīna. Hanging out with anyone and everyone I could meet filling up all my time with adventure. With my soul family. I was presented with the life that I dreamed of having for myself. I took a backseat on the self care thinking I was mastery. So foolish of me to think that way. I was spending more time on everything else outside of myself when the universe once again slapped me in the face. I was out surfing one day when I began to think in my head per usual. I sat up on my board, legs dragging in the water beneath me. It occurred to me how stressed out I felt. How I was distracting myself with surfing. I had so many other responsibilities that needed taking care of. As I lay back down to paddle for a wave I think to myself, I am going to relax and take some time to myself to get my life in order when I feel a sharp burning sensation come across my left forearm. I thought something had bit me, but the burning continued to grow stronger. I lifted my arm to the sight of bright blue tentacles wrapping around the edge of my wrist. It was hot and stinging the skin off fast. I began to scream. Pulling the sticking jelly substance off as a wave came crashing down. There it was a man-of-war jellyfish. As the wave crashed the flying bits landed across my face hitting the bridge of my nose and cheek. I could not feel my arm. It had wrapped its whole body around my wrist up to my armpit. I was afraid to paddle, I was not going to get stung again. I was in an insurmountable amount of pain and all I could do was laugh and sob at the same time. I was laughing because I knew that I was too distracted, and this was spirit's way of telling me to slow down...again. The jellyfish sting was the last time that I would succumb to distraction in regard to the task with this book. Why keep setting myself up to get slapped in the face by 2x4's? It was time to balance and listen to what I needed to do. What did I need to do? Finish writing this book.

Hurricane Douglas

Without the proper understanding, which I did not have at the time, we can let our energy run loose. Imagine that energy like a walking firecracker shooting loose sparks all rampant. Completely unaware at the time that this could happen I woke up, did my yoga and daily meditation. 5:55 on the clock. I had never seen different sets of numbers throughout the summer it had only been the 11's. This day I felt like Bradley Cooper in limitless. My intuition was near perfect. My timing was just right for everything, right as I finished my yoga practice for the day, I received a text from a friend, "wanna go surfing?" We paddled out on the glassy water. Euphoria without substance. The sky as close as a bedroom ceiling resembling something like the wallpaper from Toy Story. The water, the most cushioned blue glossing in the sunshine. Real glitter cascading like twinkling bulbs spreading across the space that the sunlight reached out. I jumped off my board into the water and emerged into the feeling between the pull of the ocean and the air. For a brief moment I was cocooned inside a water bubble until the air penetrated from the top encasing me in oxygen. The clouds had shifted and appeared to be giving me a thumbs up. I was catching every wave. My brain was operating at what felt like superior capacity and I truly felt limitless. Again, this feeling of divine appreciation settled into my being. I was filled with oneness. I was humbled by every possible amount of gratitude that could fit into a person my size. It dawned on me that I was alive on this beautiful planet, getting thumbs up from angels in the clouds. The best way I could put it drunk off grace. Source love. After the surfing session I checked the time as I arrived back to my treehouse and it was none other than 2:22… Something epic was happening. There is no doubt in my mind I was accessing damn near full consciousness in my waking life that day. Everything seemed to flow a little too perfectly. My timing, the feelings, the effortless effort that was taking over control of my personality. I could feel it. I was fulfilling the true path. Riding high off source love I came to an abrupt pause as it caught my attention how dark the sky had turned. I had not watched a lick of news since I arrived on the island and had no idea that there was a hurricane on its way. Hurricane Douglas. Hurricane's that hit the islands often break apart and nobody seemed to be concerned. Even as the sky grew grayer and scarier people played in the ocean as if it were a bright and sunny Saturday. The sky lighting up in colors that nobody else seemed to see no matter how many times I would ask. At this point I knew that the more often I saw things in the skies the less likely it was that anyone else was seeing it. It was my crazy and as confused by it as I was at the time, I loved it. I knew the energy was shifting in the world. Light beings were waking up everywhere and the energy was from more than a swirling storm in the middle of the Pacific. As there is no such thing as a coincidence, I receive a text from a professor whom I really connected with from Penn State.

Also named Douglas. He taught a sustainability course at Penn

State and was the only professor I ever found to be relatable. His class so transformative in my life. He was brought into my life to introduce me to a friend. A colleague who was exactly the person I needed to speak to. When I googled him, I found his book on the unlearning process. About waking up to our consciousness! There were always people out there just like me I just hadn't known how to seek it out. Penn State was always going to be a part of my plan. Maybe that's why I resisted it so hard in High School. Part of me knew that I would always have to go there. Part of me knew that the very thing I resisted was because I was not yet ready to explore that path yet. It is my strong belief that there are certain checkpoints that we all must hit during our lifetime where we cross paths with certain people. The decisions we make all leading us to them in one way or another. This school was part of my divine plan and it felt so good to know that I had made the right decision. It was 4:44 and I was on my bike heading to the grocery store to stock up before the hurricane poured down. People were smiling and coming out of nowhere to wave to me. Limitless. I felt like I was running with the wind. In the super zone or something. Someone handed me a flower as I neared a crowd of kids my age. I hear someone flamboyantly shout at me from across the parking lot "LOVE your energy!" It felt good to hear someone else confirming my feeling for the day. I loved my energy too. As I pulled up to the bike kickstand I knew before it even happened. I lived in two parallel timelines but chose the one with a less harsh outcome. I saw myself falling but before I could fall in real time, I gracefully switched my legs to sit down softly rather than scraping up my knee. I picked myself up casually off the ground realizing that I had predicted the moment. My life was getting far too interesting for even me to handle. I waltzed into the store but wound up feeling was quite overwhelmed. Interesting characters of people began approaching me. Energy vampires. These people did not have the highest intent for me. Leeches. Like moths to a lamp the lost souls were drawn to my high spiritual energetic light. I had shivers all up and down my spine the entire time I was in the store. I grew cold and anxious. I did even want to be looked at by anyone in the store. I ran out of there without getting any groceries in a panic. The dark and strange characters that I crossed paths with were not evil, just lost. Stuck in the lower vibrations of the world and it left me feeling exhausted. Confused, I asked the universe, "What just happened to me? Who were those people? Why did I feel so high and now I feel so scarily low?" She answered. I had opened-up my third eye a little too wide. I was unprepared and did not understand how to retain my ability keeping the energy within just as much as I could project it out. I needed protection.

If all that energy could be syphoned so easily, I needed to find a way to better direct that energy toward something that would better shield myself from the energy I could not control. I sought out other self-help books but found my own way that worked for me. I found crystals and jewelry to wear. Charmed it with my energy so that I always felt protected.

But in all honesty, it always comes down to mind over matter. Sure, it feels great to wear charms. Be surrounded by crystals. Wear protective essential oils or my grandmother's carnelian ring. But at the end of the day we can create anything we want with our own mind. I learned to caress my own energy with a veil. A golden light that bubbled around me protecting me from any possible harm. Anything that would shield me from any energy that was not my own. Whenever I forgot and failed to take the time to protect my space, I felt a loss of control. I suffered for not preparing my energy field properly and learned my lesson the hard way. I hope that this reaches you in time for you to be able to prepare a little better than I had been. Tapping into the collective zeitgeist is crazy but necessary to understand the contrast, so do not be afraid. I know the difference now because when I am unprotected, I feel overly groggy. My body aches. The contrast helps in learning to develop boundaries. To envision the energy flowing through us like a cup. An overflowing cup and not a cup with holes in it. Opening the third eye feels like a mini gremlin poking out of the forehead. It's the real-world eye. The portal to all worlds and is not something to play around with. It's sacred and connects us to the higher and lower realms of the planet. Guard your eye and take care of it. Prepare your energy and awaken yourself.

X

The first test

RIENDS WHO SEND mail are the best kinds of friends. A friend from Pennsylvania was kind enough to send me a few things she thought I might need which included some crystals. Peacock ore was one of them. A decadent black stone with rainbow scratches lining the edges of the rock. Just like a peacock's fanning colorful feathers. A few moments later I checked my phone only to notice an advertisement for a production company with a peacock as its logo. Package in hand I began my trek up to my treehouse. A feather, an actual peacock feather. As there are no such thing as coincidences, I was splendidly pleased to receive the gift of my next spirit animal. New lessons, my next level up. Peacocks are an excellent symbol for recognizing the inner beauty within. A peacock's large and beautiful colors cannot be spread far and wide without a strong foundation. These animals are fierce and have extremely strong feet. Balance is found through the roots and grounding was something I needed. My energy was flying rampant all over the place and I did not know how to keep it in, but it was all due to the fact that I was not grounded. Encouraging self-love was what the peacock brought for me. Not that I did not feel beautiful, but I was not flaunting my feathers in the way that I could. I was afraid of the too much's in life. Too quiet, too loud. Too conservative, too raunchy. Too nice, too mean. I had always felt like I was too much for people. I had too much energy, and too much sass. Being told we are too much can make us feel like the muchness is not good enough. We are born to be different and stand out. That's what a peacock does. They are born to make an entrance. I put up a judgement wall of myself for a really long time. I was living in fear of being too much and not enough for anyone including myself. Another level up with the guidance of the peacock to help me learn how to flaunt my feathers a little bit. How to be confident in the body that I was born into. The energy had me flying by the seat of my pants. I was finally posting and talking about all that I wanted to talk about on my social media. I was surpassing the judgment blocks I put up for myself for so long. I was proud for the first time in my life to be exactly who I was. Unapologetically me. The peacock's energy was a lot more present than my other spirit animals. I was evolving quicker and settling into a flirty groove within myself. The true flow. We all have spirit guides to help us get through them if we are attuning to the way of life and listening to the signs of the universe, we can call upon our guides to help us in traversing the lessons. The obstacles that are put in front of us are there because we have free will. We always have the choice in making the morally correct decision in the matter. The universe is constantly checking in to make sure we are listening. To make sure that we are making the morally correct decision. The one in highest alignment with our path. Testing our devotion and trust. After hurricane Douglas I finally understood what was happening. I saw the bigger picture and gained more pieces to my puzzle. I was an empath, a psychic, a light worker. I was magical and I was special. Before I was worried about the dark energy vampires and crazy feelings in the collective. But the universe reminded me of how protected I was after a short sunset swim. The wind swirled around me almost pushing me up the street faster like I needed to get somewhere. Deep rich hues caressed the horizon beaming a bright green light at the separation beyond seeing capacity. I gazed up to the cloud formations above me to see angels dancing in plain sight. Clouds in the sky that looked just like angels with trumpets. Something like a Christmas tree ornament. It was getting dark when I turned to walk back when I was approached by a man named Angel. It was as if this person was not a person at all. The only thing that I can remember of what he said was "there is no need to worry, you must have a lot of guardian angels." There was no reason to be afraid. I was going to continue with my purpose regardless of the darkness that was arising. I was being heavily guarded by angels and had no reason to fear. During this time, I felt the dragging desire to meditate more than once every day. I began meditating three times a day and began feeling the effects. My body was changing and so was my brain. My experiences were enhancing, and life started to get even weirder. Weird in the most exciting way possible.

Ascending

I had always been a highly sensitive person, but I had no way of getting in touch with the things that I was feeling or picking up on. I was always called out for being too sensitive, but now it is my strength. Sensitivity is connectivity. Us highly sensitive people can learn to hone in on every possible thing that we might be feeling. HSP's are empaths. People who are capable of detecting a far and rather, larger scope of emotions that surround us. Sensing deeper than the 3D reality and tapping into the 4th, 5th, 6th and 7th dimensions. Empaths are psychologically sensitive to the energies that surround a person or situation. Anyone can certainly feel empathy for a situation but empaths will physically take on the symptoms of someone around them that might be hurt. Will physically take on the emotions and feelings of others around them. Us HSP's are not broken machines we are extremely intelligent, mislabeled light rays capable of changing the world. How can we transcend duality? I think that ascension is achievable in this lifetime. How is it going to be possible to transcend duality! The earth is full of opposite. Full of fear just as much as it is love. But it is going to take every single person on this earth facing their own duality. Humans are innately competitive by nature. We are social creatures seeking to belong. Well imagine what it would be like to wake up one day to see every single person around you experiencing something that you weren't... experiencing evolution. Experiencing waking up. Waking up happens one day but it happens because we choose to pull ourself away from the ego. We lose another sense of individual self-identity by choosing gratitude. Choosing forgiveness. Choosing kindness and love. We can upgrade our DNA by being light. Stop carrying the burdens of hate, resentment, fear, guilt, shame. Evolve! Run, walk, swim, dance your way into healing yourself. Because the only way to teach is to act and not to preach. It's hard to face duality. People are judgmental. People do not understand. But that is the ultimate truth. It is not about hiding, it is about loving. This new earth will never come to fruition the more we hide. Every empath knows that it's hard to go in public because the pressure is hard. Being sensitive to other people is hard. But that is why we develop our aura. Why we get stronger, better, closer to healing. It is not about hiding anymore, we have to face our shit. We have to love ourself for where we are just as much as where we are going. We have to love until we cannot possibly love any less. We cannot force anyone to do anything, we can only just be. But remember, the more loving you are the more they will ask. They more they will wonder just how you do it. How you love so much! Evolution is grand. It's rising. No one will want to be left behind. Ascension, is possible because love always wins. We are alive for some of the most peaceful times on this planet. The transition birthing the new world into light. I was given a gift, shown and channeled the new world. What it would feel like. What it would look like for me. I knew what was waiting for me if I kept pressing onward. Working out all of my kinks. The bad habits and triggering emotional patterns which were keeping me in the 3-D. What I saw in this vision was my child picking an apple off the counter as she ran straight into the most beautiful backyard. It was not a past life, this was my lifetime. I saw the love of my life sitting next to me, laughing about something in the sand. I was at peace. I was truly, home. I was given the gift of a promise that if I kept working on myself I would achieve all that I ever wanted in this lifetime. I walked through an orchard. It was a future friend of mine. There was so much warmth from the sun, and the rain perfectly tending to the growing garden surrounding us. We could grow anything because the land was healed. We spoke and communicated with the land. Food was growing not only in the ground but magically in the sky. I touched the wood in my house, it was fresh. We built it. We were near water where we could go surfing. I turned a corner of the house to reveal the most intricately carved yellow board. The design looked to be carved of light language. This was my why, why I kept writing this book even when I felt crazy. When I didn't understand what was happening to me. When

I doubted myself that nobody might read it. The numbers were there to remind me that it was perfect. I was doing my part. The gifts, oh the gracious gifts. Divine appreciation, and pure source love. As we grow into our sensitivity and rewire our consciousness we begin to ascend. We rewrite the imprints on our DNA which were passed down from generations. We upgrade our human experience. Ascension is the process of surrender. It's the light which carries through within us. This process of evolution i speak of, when you think about it we're progressing along the trend line of growth up into the higher dimensions. From hunter gatherers-forward to present and onward to humanity's future. Operating first out of fear and on our way to love in the 4th and 5th dimensions. This love leading to unity consciousness. A complete resolution and preparation for limitless existence. This is the truth all people seek to define. The undefinable truth which is only known through the process of evolving. Through the process of surrender to the utmost ability. The only oneness and nakedness that represents our true being. Who we really are. During my ascension process I felt as though my limbs were ripping apart. I was sleeping enough but still so exhausted. I couldn't stop eating either. All my body wanted was peanut butter sandwiches. I ate two day sometimes then would continue to shove my spoon into the peanut butter jar on throughout the day. I finished probably four or five peanut butter jars that week. Comfort food. I was craving fat for the weight. I was eating so much because my body felt the need to protect itself. To keep the weight on because my DNA was practically flying out of my own body. I was not grounded. I barely could interact with anyone for longer than five minutes without feeling groggy. They call it ascension flu. All my energy was drained no matter what remedy I implemented on myself. Tea, proper sleep, meditation, food. Then the dreams started. I was having very vivid nightmares two or three times a night. Every night someone that I had previously had some sort of close relationship with would show up in my dream somewhere along the way. It was fun being able to connect with the relationships that I missed, but it felt wrong. Every time I was seeing those connections, I would get attacked. These hovering, black clothed skeletons would come to drown me every night after reconnecting with friends in my sleep. Around the time I was having these vivid nightmares I came to run into exactly the person who could help me understand what was happening. A quantum hypnotherapist. There are so many different types of healing in this world, but this was the fast track. I could skip years of therapy, dozens of massages and acupuncture sessions to work out the trauma which still very much did exist in my body. I only needed one session. The reason why I was having the strange dreams was because I was still attached in the quantum field to people that were not raising their vibes. My energy was still being shared elsewhere with those people even though I moved halfway across the world. In quantum physics energy can be borrowed and in relationships our energies can intertwine themselves getting caught up in knot after knot. This is called quantum entanglement. The reason why we just 'know' things when our close family or friends are up to no good is because of quantum entanglement. During the session with the hypnotist this and other truths came to surface. I had karmic debt that needed to be paid and quantum cords that needed to be cut. There was still healing that needed to be patched up in order for me to keep accelerating through my spiritual path. The confusion and questions were answered. I knew what I had to do. I was finally free, and the future was so close. The numbers began suffocating me at this point with how often I was viewing the synchronicities. 2:22, 4:44, 5:55

it was one after another anytime I checked the clock or moved to the next thing I was seeing so many signs. I would check the clock at perfect numbers. 7:22, 4:55. My phone or laptop would end up at 77% or 11% whenever I would gaze to check the battery. I would find feathers every day at my door, or in my walking path. I was guided and very protected because I was listening. Leaves were swirling all around me as I walked outside my door down the stairs. I thought I was dreaming. I felt exuberantly confident for some reason. Every time I looked in the mirror, I saw my soul glowing inside of me. I had been guided by spirit animals all this time, angels, my grandparents. It was all unfolding perfectly. I began to hear whistling in my ears when no one was around. Low- and high-pitched ear ringing. I began to sense my surroundings at a more heightened awareness. Spirits were everywhere. The earth was beautiful like it was when I was a kid. Amazed at everything once again. The smallest of things surprised me. My spirit was so happy. I was beaming with grace and truly walking with God. Streetlights would flicker in my presence. Radio stations would tune in and out as I would step into friends' cars. My aura and magnetic field growing. Filled with love and light. I was living and breathing for the first time all over again. Divine appreciation is so different than anything I had ever felt. An awoken soul can have this feeling of divine appreciation when they are fully present in the moment. Fully one with the earth andspirit. This is unity consciousness. We can grab glimpses of this feeling in our process of evolving because the ego dissipates and all we operate out of are presentness, oneness, and limitlessness. The triple crowning of unifying energy. Full flow. It's euphoric and feels like the start of a psychedelic trip. It's orgasmic appreciation. It is not love, it's source love which extends far beyond in any of the depths of time and space. I am not sure that there are

English words that can be put to the equivalent of the feeling. It's a submerging of the heart so true, it's the deepest truth. It's the hand of god holding onto your soul. It's the grace of source kissing your heart. It's sweet and serene like fresh fruit from a tree. Divine appreciation is something that is the closest that we can get in this lifetime incarnated on earth to pureness. To nothingness and everything that is consciousness. This feeling was inspiring, I felt the track pulling me forward. I was waking up to my full power even though I did not know how to use it yet. My full consciousness. With every step I took I grew closer to my purpose and my fate on this earth. The numbers there as a reminder from our guides that yes, you are doing the right thing. Listening and making the decisions most aligned with the path. The gifts were to reward me for my efforts in changing the person who I was by shattering old habits and opening my heart space to the truth, reminding me that anything is possible. The guidance continues now to grow, and I feel as if all the little moments are useless to keep layering in this book. If you made it this far and are still skeptical of this magical world. Then you have a lot of work to do. What is it about resistance? The way it is always exactly what we need to focus on, that is the very thing that we run away from. We resist some beliefs as a protection mechanism. The law of motion states that for every action there is an equal but opposite reaction. No big dream, result that we want, desire, can be overcome without resistance. The greater the dream the greater the resistance. The more magical you are the more likely you are to resist the very thing that you are afraid of. We resist by disbelieving first because it has not happened to us so therefore it is false and can never become part of our reality. Maybe we begin to believe but obstacles begin to present themselves in the form of questions. We stare at it and wonder how is this possible? Why is it happening? Why does this not make sense? We create blocks. We procrastinate, we forget, we ignore, we suppress, we are afraid. We are afraid of being powerful beyond what we can measure ourselves. We are afraid that we actually might do it, we might get everything that we ever wanted. Afraid of who we truly are. IF there is anything that three generations of Star Wars movies taught me, it's that in order to defeat the empire we must stop being afraid of who we are. That we are the darkness as much as we are the light. Face the resistance in life. What are we protecting ourselves from?

The gifts

Clairessences. The essence of being clear. Everyone is completely capable of being psychic. I was tossing and turning one night, which usually meant my angels are trying to let me know something. So I hop on my phone, I hear some thoughts start to make their way into my brain and as I typed in a p a school on the island showed up. A psychic school. My ears rang like the playing of a gong. I reached out to the school and found that I could start training and accessing my abilities by taking courses with teachers who could help me through all of the random bits and pieces that were happening to me. Maybe I act throughout this book as if I knew what was going on, but the best part is the entire time I had no idea what was going on. I was getting thrown into situations left and right. My experiences were all over the place and it never seemed to match up with anyone around me until I began to see clearly. Clairessence, the essence of being clear. Experiencing life clearly entails so many of our senses and beyond what we understand to be the 'normal' human experience. Clairessence is the nature of being any one or all of the energy readers. In middle school I still recall the day that I was picked to be the oracle of Delphi in class. Our seventh- grade teacher put all of us into a hat when we were learning about the romans and mythology. I wanted to be the oracle so bad and to my surprise I got it. I sat in the closet of the classroom with my crystal ball and cards. I got to 'predict' people's future and hide in the closet for the first fifteen or so minutes of class. I was to wait in there until those who had earned money doing various other learning tasks decided to use it to pay a visit in the oracles lair. I was always going to be magical like the oracle. Clairessence is a magnificent thing, which we all can tap into if we choose to hone in on this skill in the brain. We can be clairsentient (clear feeling), clairvoyant (clear seeing), clairgustant (clear tasting), and clairaudient (clear hearing). All of which began to amplify in my life. Again, thinking I was absolutely insane I was experiencing all of it. Seeing spirits in nature. Feeling the colors, and not just seeing them. I was hearing in color. Hearing white noise and various pitches float in through my ears. Angels reminding me that they were there. Voices that were not mine in my head floating by like gentle whispers. It was magical. It was real. It was the part of life that I had yet to experience. I was finally seeing clearly for the first time. The world that we see is not made of anything but chaos. The veil no longer existed, and I was walking with the other side. I heard the essence of life beyond and was never going to turn back. Spirits whistling in my ear asking me to play. To dance around upon the magical earth. Up until that point I never knew my potential to be so strong. This was how I was going to help people; this was the way. I knew I was an empath.

I knew I was connected and psychic. I was so powerful, and I could not wait for people to see me for who I was. Who my grandmother was even though the world around her was not ready yet. I was not going to deteriorate I was breaking the chain and stepping into my full power. Source blessed me every single day reminding me that it was okay by presenting gifts. Physical gifts. Feathers began to show up every day. Every single day as I grew further away from my shadow and closer to the light. I was liberated by my newfound love for the world. For all the things I did know just as much as the things that I didn't. I walked around like I was the shit because normal people had no idea how powerful I was. I splashed and played with the magic in the clouds. I walked along nature like I was a part of it, not against it. I again found myself singing with the birds and laughing with the trees. I was touched by warm grace. Raw source love. Divine appreciation. One walk back on a casual afternoon I approach a tall but dark and handsome young man throw a chair into the back of his red ford ranger. Interested in the vibes I said hello.

He was going to read on the beach, so I tagged along with him and two others. There really is nothing like a truck in Hawai'i.

Bouncing and rebounding off the potholes in the roads. Warm island air blowing through the windows. Tires screeching barely hanging on to the rims. We were all messing around poking fun at each other on the beach when one of the friends that had come with us was ranting about her inability to focus. I felt the urge to grab her hands, that was all I did. Grab her hands and she began looking at me so strange. As I gazed with a comforting smile into her eyes, I told her, "everything is going to be alright" we sat there for a moment. In my head I thought "SEND HER LOVE" and that was it. Lost in the trance she started to tear up. I was feeling something flow through. She asked, "what are you doing to me?" I had no idea what it even was. I let go of her hands and she shook her head a bit. She began looking at everything really strange, like the way that people do when they are tripping on psychedelics. "The colors are so much more vibrant, abbey what did you just do?" I had no idea what I did. The warm sensation and brief pause happened so slowly that it was hard to even know what was happening. What happened? I asked source what happened that day and was gifted with a book...A book on Reiki! The universal healing art restoring emotional and physical wellbeing. I was a healer and I finally found part of my true purpose. I was here to heal, and this was part of my gifts to humanity. My purpose like all of us here on earth was to heal. I gathered all the pieces to the puzzle, all that I needed to do was put them in place.

XI

What it takes to get there

THE BUTTERFLY SPIRIT animal appeared in my dreams. A bright and ravishingly flittering angel appeared right before I woke up. They followed me wherever I went. I noticed them flittering right alongside me as if our souls were having conversations I was not aware of. The butterfly's energy was forcing me into my next unfolding transition. The beautiful metamorphosis, another level up. I awoke something inside of myself. More than the awakening I began with. I was given my gifts in a space beyond what I thought to be reality. I was a true healer. Being alive was real. Being me was real and I was special. I was different.

I was, finally, me. Figuring out who we are is who we always were before all the shit. Before the fear. Before the trauma. Before we lost the person we were always meant to be. I was healing the inner child which had succumbed to cynicism in life because of the trauma. This adventure was my chrysalis before my transformation into a starling butterfly. Monarch butterflies are stronger than they look. They fly straight into thunderstorms because they have such a long migration, they can't waste any time stopping for shelter. They are brave because they fly into the danger. That was exactly what I was doing. Flying straight into the storm I hadn't seen coming. I was nestling in to my new home on the island. I felt at peace. I felt love and my true self was beaming, that is until the message arrived. A friend and I were sorting through some things in her garage as she he interrupts, "you are going to go home and forgive your mother. Heal and love your family." I blinked and thought... Excuse me? We were talking about bikini bottoms and she brought up my mother for absolutely no reason at all. Someone in heaven had used her voice and spoken directly to me. This was not what I wanted. I did not want to leave the island. I wanted to stay and live out my happiest life. But there was something I needed to do in regards to my healing. My family. The truth that I needed to speak to them. They had no idea who I was. It was time to fly into the storm. My last week was all the more special than ever before. I met more magical friends and went on so many more magical adventures that have to be saved for a different story. My parting gift from the land was something that I get to wear around my chest, my heart, every single day reminding me of my true home. It was my last day and I went to the food truck around the corner from my place to get one last meal only to have crossed paths with a kind young gentleman offering me a coconut. We talked story for moment when he invited me to his shell lounge, as interesting as a phrase that is it actually happened. I knew that no harm could possibly come out of this experience. So many beautiful shells. Such an amazing treasure to be able to see such beautiful colors. Beautiful pieces of art that the earth provides for us. Some of earth's rarest of treasures. Sunrise shells are native to the waters of the island. Each one shedding beautiful rays of pink, yellow, orange, and purple light similar to a beautiful sunrise. In Hawaiian legend, these shells were worn by royalty and I certainly felt the land radiating with my heartbeat. Feeling her love inside this small shell. Her gifts and memories she brought to me. My truest home where I belong. Even though I was heading to my birth home where new obstacle and tests of faith erupted. Thunder booming in front of my wings as I raced into the storm of chaos that was the mainland. Fear. Anger. Disgust. Hate. I felt it all in a craze, the flight home was filled with anxious and confused human beings. But I was following the path and listening to the call. I was protected and I was learning that the flight home was only the beginning. I was different but the world seemed to be the same. Nothing had changed from when I got back except my parents' confusion.

They had absolutely no idea who their daughter was. They were hateful because I was not who I used to be. Confused as to how I changed that fast. My parents thought that I was crazy. Insane.

Thinking I had joined a cult and been completely brainwashed. Coming home, I realized that nobody understood any part of the person that I had become. I was unsupported by my family.

They were so angry and frustrated. They didn't understand. But that was part of the process. Awakening to the truth and fully letting go of control. Releasing the idea that maybe they might not ever understand and it was not my job to wake them up. Sure, they were aware. But they were not quite awake. It hurt a lot to think that the people I loved were lost but could so easily find themselves. But some souls don't want that for themselves. Some souls are not ready which is why we must refrain from judgement. We can only be our truest and most authentic selves for others to awaken. To express consciousness is that of a radiant embodiment of light. Of purpose. I knew my purpose and was charging steadfast on alignment. I was ready. Everything I had ever learned was to get me right here. All the pieces of the puzzle I had collected. The challenges, the love, and the light I found within myself were perfect. I loved who I was. FUCK it felt, and still feels so good to be me. There are not even words which I can fully communicate with myself to express the profound wonder of the universe. My heart was finally fully open. I no longer felt the need to keep it to myself. I did not need to shut anyone out. I found the happiness within myself. Happiness in being purposeful. Life itself isn't about happiness because ultimately happiness can be quite a selfish way to live. When we seek happiness it is for none other than the self. When we seek to be useful, to be helpful to others is when we are truly fulfilled. When we become truly honorable and compassionate to have made a difference in somebody else's journey outside of our own. I found it. I found my purpose. All that it took to get here. I followed my heart and I listened to the call. I found the truest me. How do we get here? Together. It is so excruciatingly necessary that the light beings of this earth shake up the ground beneath our feet. Break through the uncomfortable ways of our pasts and fully embrace the people we are. FULLY and unapologetically. Full surrender to the self and source. Full trust in the guidance that is laid out for us. Trust that the universe knows what is best for us. For whatever it is that we try to control is exactly the resistance we create around getting the life that we so desire. The ultimate test of service comes from full surrender. Toward achieving peace on earth. I do not believe things anymore. I know. I know that the light is here and it's glowing brighter and brighter every day like the warmth that could come from thousands of angels singing. Life was great before. It was like everyone else I knew. It was so fucking normal it hurts. It was comfortable until I fully let go. Put every ounce of trust I had into the divine even though it did not seem to make any sense at times. When I relinquished the last bit of control I had over my life the magic became real. All of the clues and blurry details became clear. All of the subtle hints were suddenly murals painted on a city street wall. I was never meant to fit in. I was never meant to be fully understood. That was always going to be part of my process. Part of my story to tell. I spent so much time running away from who I truly was which was so much lonelier than being alone. It isn't our job to make anyone see. It is not our responsibility to help anyone understand even if that means our own family. Everyone has a role to play, a purpose. A purpose in their story and walk of life. Where we were is exactly the place someone else is searching fo. Someone that is where we are now. When we share our stories, we mend what is fragmented so that we can keep on healing. Maybe all of the stories will connect the dots. The more stories we share the closer we grow together in healing. To inspire one another to keep on living. We have the power to keep on writing our story because we are all authors of our own book of life. We are the directors of our own movie. The scientist in our lab. We play the melody that sings our song on earth. The best stories are the ones that work out all the details. The best ones take time and commitment to make. The best stories are the ones that reveal truth. Only by the means of seeking our own truths will we ever be able to set ourselves free. Free from the pain, the war, the injustice, the racism, the abuse, the illness, the hate, the anger, and the fear that pushes us further away from one another. When we seek out the truth, we find alignment in the power of knowledge. The more we know, we come to find more we don't know. But we don't have to know everything, our goal is to pursue our highest truth of what we do know. Share our story. By sharing we not only elevate those who feel they might not have anyone to relate to, but we also elevate ourselves. When we speak, we carry with us the power of all those who lived before us. The stories from our ancestors who have always been waiting for someone to break the chain and tell this truth. We cannot control all of the external ever-changing environments in our lives but what we can control are how we make others feel and what actions we take with our time. I used to put so much pressure on my life worrying about all of the problems that existed in the world and how I was going to fix them. All the deep cuts I felt, humans hurting other humans. Humans hurting the earth and other spirits living upon it. All those burdens were not mine to carry, nor were they a part of my story. I did not grow up along a coastline where my home was destroyed because of erosion, as much as I wanted to go and heal the soil from all powerful climate change catastrophe's it was not my truth to tell. I did not grow up as a minority combatting racism and discrimination, as hard as I felt for all of my close friends who struggled from the systems keeping them so oppressed it was not my truth to tell. I grew up as me, with my own baggage and own truths to unfold. There is this quote by an old Persian poet, Rumi, that says, "Yesterday I am clever, so I wanted to change the world. Today I am wise, so I am changing myself." Understanding this might seem paradoxical, when there is so much to care about in the world that seems to need fixing. It seems so selfish. But the truth is, the more energy we put into healing ourselves the more energy the earth can put into healing herself. The more energy everyone can put into growing their being. Our own personal journey that is not like anyone else's. Again, and again finding home in the space of being alone. We will never truly be at home until we find the stillness within our self. We decided to reincarnate on earth agreeing to the hardships that life puts us through. The beautiful love affair, the circle of life. We lose ourselves in hopes that we are strong enough to find it again. Everyone has a roll to play. Even those who are not awake. The yin and yang. Every being is full of light. Even those who play with the dark. Everyone owns a purpose for that story to be unfolded. A purpose for telling that story and speaking love when it is their time. SPEAK your truth. Seek out what it is that you desire and run for the hills. Break down the barriers. Fill yourself with light and love. I challenge you to be brave in sharing your story and all that it took for you to get exactly where you are. The whole world is waiting. This cosmos is a magical place. I found myself and maybe someday you will find that you too, get here.

Afterword

I PROFESS A PROFOUND amount of gratitude for all of the people I met along the way. The people who challenged me, the people who made me feel unloved as much as those who made me feel love. For all of the experiences that I was so fortunate to have. I was always so loved and so blessed for every single thing. Always so guided. So loved. I am forever grateful. Without any of you, I would never have been able to get here without everyone together. Thank you.